*Short Bike Rides™ Series*

# Short Bike Rides™ in Eastern Pennsylvania

### Fourth Edition

*by* Bill Simpson

D1310177

The Globe Pequot Press

Old Saybrook, Connecticut

Cover photo: Chris Dubé
Cover design: Saralyn D'Amato-Twomey

The photo on page 58 was taken by Joe Surkiewicz. All other photos are by the author.

Library of Congress Cataloging-in-Publication Data
Simpson, Bill, 1950–
    Short bike rides in eastern Pennsylvania / by Bill Simpson. —4th ed.
        p.    cm.  — (Short bike rides series)
    ISBN 0-7627-0206-0
    1. Bicycle touring—Pennsylvania—Guidebooks.  2. Pennsylvania—Guidebooks.  I. Title.  II. Series.
GV1045.5.P4S56  1998
917.48—DC21                    97-47210
                                              CIP

Manufactured in the United States of America
Fourth Edition/First Printing

# Contents

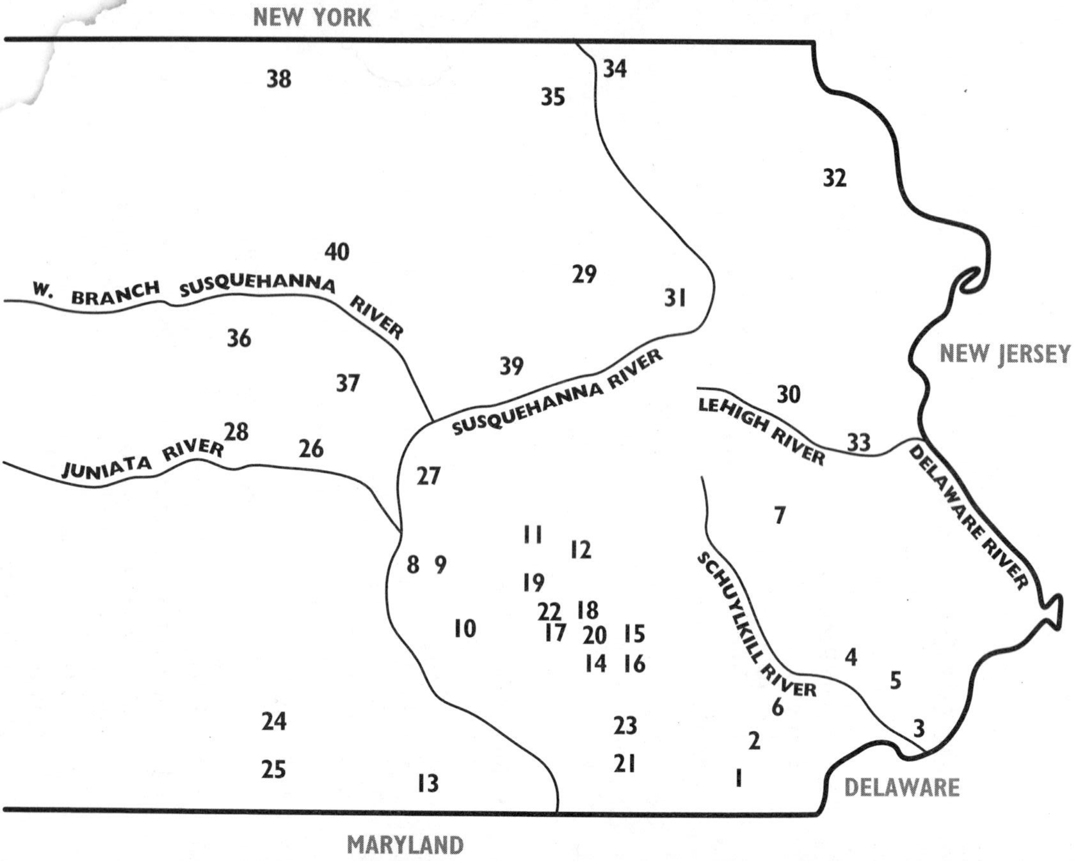
NEW YORK
38
35
34
32
40
W. BRANCH SUSQUEHANNA RIVER
29
31
36
39
37
NEW JERSEY
SUSQUEHANNA RIVER
30
28
26
JUNIATA RIVER
LEHIGH RIVER
33
DELAWARE RIVER
27
7
11
12
8
9
19
SCHUYLKILL RIVER
22
18
10
17
20
15
14
16
4
5
6
24
23
2
3
25
21
1
13
DELAWARE
MARYLAND

## Ridge and Valley Region

## Northeast Region

## North Central Region

| | Romantic | Historic | Educational |
|---|---|---|---|
| **1** Atglen | ● | | |
| **2** Downingtown | | | |
| **3** Philadelphia | | ● | ● |
| **4** Valley Forge | | ● | |
| **5** Valley Forge to Philadelphia | | ● | |
| **6** French Creek | | ● | |
| **7** Trexlertown | | | ● |
| **8** Harrisburg | | ● | ● |
| **9** Hershey | ● | | ● |
| **10** Marietta | | | |
| **11** Fredericksburg | | | |
| **12** Myerstown | | | |
| **13** New Freedom | ● | | |
| **14** Bird-In-Hand | | | |
| **15** Blue Ball | ● | | |
| **16** Intercourse | ● | | |
| **17** Lancaster Co. Cover'd Bridges | ● | ● | ● |
| **18** Middle Creek | | | |
| **19** Mount Gretna/Mount Hope | ● | | |
| **20** New Holland | | | ● |
| **21** Quarryville | ● | | |
| **22** Speedwell Forge | | | |
| **23** Strasburg | | ● | |
| **24** Biglerville | ● | | ● |
| **25** Gettysburg | | ● | ● |
| **26** Newport | | | |
| **27** Millersburg | ● | ● | ● |
| **28** Thompsontown | ● | | |
| **29** Eagles Mere | ● | | |
| **30** Eckley | | ● | ● |
| **31** Harveys Lake | | | |
| **32** Honesdale | | ● | |
| **33** Jim Thorpe | ● | ● | |
| **34** Athens | | ● | |
| **35** Canton | | | |
| **36** Loganton | ● | | |
| **37** Penn's Creek | | ● | ● |
| **38** Wellsboro | ● | | |
| **39** Washingtonville | | ● | |
| **40** Montoursville | | | |

| Scenic | Relaxing | Rural | Easy | Challenging | |
|:---:|:---:|:---:|:---:|:---:|:---:|
| ● | | | | | **1** |
| | ● | | ● | | **2** |
| | | | | | **3** |
| | ● | | | | **4** |
| | ● | | ● | | **5** |
| ● | | | | ● | **6** |
| ● | | ● | | ● | **7** |
| | | | | | **8** |
| | | | | | **9** |
| ● | | ● | | | **10** |
| ● | | ● | | | **11** |
| ● | | ● | | | **12** |
| ● | ● | | ● | | **13** |
| ● | | ● | | | **14** |
| ● | | ● | | | **15** |
| ● | | ● | | | **16** |
| ● | | | | | **17** |
| ● | | ● | | ● | **18** |
| ● | | | | ● | **19** |
| ● | | ● | | ● | **20** |
| ● | | ● | | ● | **21** |
| ● | | | | ● | **22** |
| ● | | ● | | ● | **23** |
| ● | | | | | **24** |
| ● | | | | | **25** |
| ● | ● | ● | | | **26** |
| ● | | | | | **27** |
| ● | | ● | | | **28** |
| ● | | | | ● | **29** |
| | | | | | **30** |
| ● | ● | | ● | | **31** |
| ● | | ● | | | **32** |
| ● | ● | | ● | | **33** |
| | | | ● | | **34** |
| ● | | ● | | ● | **35** |
| ● | | ● | | | **36** |
| ● | | | | | **37** |
| ● | ● | | ● | | **38** |
| ● | | ● | | | **39** |
| | ● | | ● | | **40** |

# Introduction

Welcome to Pennsylvania. If your idea of the Keystone State is the cities of Philadelphia and Pittsburgh, some pleasant surprises await you. Pennsylvania means "Penn's Woods" and forests still cover large areas of the commonwealth. Visitors to Pennsylvania, especially those from the arid West, often express amazement at the unending green; not money but trees, grass, and crops. In the southeastern part of the state, where many of these rides take place, farming is the dominant industry. Farm areas have plenty of lightly traveled back roads, and these roads provide excellent bicycling opportunities.

Pennsylvania is a fairly big state, and that's why this book covers only the eastern half. Even so, it's well over 200 miles from New Freedom (ride 13), the southernmost ride, to Wellsboro (ride 38), the northernmost ride.

The last time anyone measured, Pennsylvania had more miles of road than any other state in the union, although California was working feverishly to pave itself into the lead. Surprisingly, Lancaster County has more miles of road than any other county in the state. Because of that, Lancaster County has a reputation as one of the ten best places in the world for recreational bicycling. Hundreds of miles of lightly traveled farm roads will earn a place in that sort of reputation. Lancaster County is one of the few places in the country where you can come to a covered bridge and encounter a traffic jam that consists of two bicycles and three horse-drawn buggies.

Most of these rides travel through rural areas. The exceptions are the Philadelphia and Harrisburg rides, and they both provide scenic river views.

In Pennsylvania you'll find varied attractions both historical and natural. Battlefields at Gettysburg and Valley Forge, historical sites such as Independence Hall and Wheatland, covered bridges, a wildlife management area at Middle Creek, the smell of chocolate in Hershey, and the beauty of the farms will delight you as you traverse the city streets and country roads of Pennsylvania.

Pennsylvania is not a flat state and these rides cover all sorts of terrain. Hill climbers will love the Mount Gretna and Eagles Mere rides while flatlanders will feel right at home at Harveys Lake and on the rail trails. Most rides include a mix of hills and flat sections. Some are sightseeing tours, and some are simply great places to get away from traffic and enjoy a leisurely ride. Several rides have long and short options, and several have opportunities to connect to other rides.

As you travel through Pennsylvania, it may be helpful to know that Pennsylvania has a two-tiered system for numbering state routes. When the route numbers are 999 or lower, the highway is a major one and the road signs are large—about 7 feet high. When the route numbers are 1000 or higher, the signs are much smaller—about 3 feet high. These carry a designation such as SR 1006 and because of their size, they're easy to miss. All references throughout this guide to the "SR" routes carry the SR prefix. References to other state routes (999 or lower) are designated by the word *Route* only; for example, Route 34.

The book is set up to make your planning and riding as simple as possible. At the beginning of each ride description, you'll find these seven categories of information:

1. Distance of ride in miles;
2. Approximate pedaling time;
3. Description of terrain;
4. Condition of road surface;
5. Things to see on the ride;
6. Where you can find food on the ride; and
7. Locations of restroom facilities.

The description of each ride tells you what to look for along the way, where to expect big hills, and the times of the year when festivals and other events take place. The directions for the rides indicate mileage at each turn. These were measured on a bike odometer and will guide you along the route.

Bicycling in Pennsylvania can be enjoyable, scenic, and challenging. Have fun and ride safely.

# Tips

*Always wear a helmet.* (Helmets are mandatory for riders under 12.)

Aside from cars, the biggest problem bikers face is dogs. Pennsylvania is no different from any other state in that respect. Especially in rural areas, people often let dogs run loose. Your best protection is some sort of spray. Tear gas carried in the back pocket of a biking shirt is ideal. It's easy to grab, and it will instantly stop Fido. But don't shoot into a strong wind.

The best times to ride are from about 9:00 A.M. to 2:00 P.M. Traffic is generally lightest then. And because many of these rides go to popular attractions, traffic is often lighter on weekdays than on weekends. Probably the best month for riding is October.

One of the most important safety devices to appear in many years came out of southeastern Pennsylvania. The VistaLite's pulsating light makes riders visible in darkness, at distances up to 2,000 feet. Long before a driver is on top of you, he'll know that something is in the road ahead. The VistaLite is the creation of a Lancaster man, Robert Choi, and it's available in bike stores everywhere.

# About the Amish

One factor that makes Lancaster and surrounding counties superb for bike riding is the Amish. The Amish are a people whose religious beliefs prohibit the use of such modern conveniences as electricity and cars. The Amish travel by horse and buggy. This creates some unusual, though very minor, road hazards. One is the ruts that the horses wear in the roads. Fortunately, the ruts are far enough from the edge of the road to leave plenty of room for a bike. The other hazard is what the locals call "road apples." These are what result when a horse has relieved itself on the road. Most riders are happy to navigate these obstacles in exchange for having the roads almost to themselves.

The Amish are friendly, but they value their privacy and will not consent to having their pictures taken. Please treat these people with respect.

# The Weather

Pennsylvania's climate has some of everything. It can be seventy-five degrees in January and freezing in April. But it's always hot in the summer. The driest months are generally September and October. In summer, rainy days are rather rare, but thunderstorms are common. They usually pop up in the late afternoon or evening and generally roll in from the west.

It would be risky to plan a biking vacation for Pennsylvania in December, January, or February, but if you're coming during those months, it can't hurt to bring your bike. Every month has at least a few good days for biking, and the snow usually melts rather quickly. Local riders rarely endure more than two weeks when they can't do some riding.

# Covered Bridges

As you pedal along on many of these rides, you'll come to covered bridges. There were once thousands of these structures in the state, but their number has dwindled tremendously. Today, approximately 230 remain in Pennsylvania. Although many people associate covered bridges with Vermont, Pennsylvania has more than any other state.

Lancaster County has more covered bridges than any other county—thirty. One ride—Lancaster County Covered Bridges (ride 17)—takes you through five of them.

Southeastern Pennsylvania can rightfully claim to be the covered-bridge capital of the nation. The first one built in the country spanned the Schuylkill in Philadelphia. The longest one ever built—5,690 feet—crossed the Susquehanna between Columbia and Wrightsville.

Riding through covered bridges requires caution. It is possible to catch a tire between the boards, so it's a good idea to walk your bike through. It's also a good idea to make sure that there are no cars in the bridge when you cross. The bridges are fairly narrow, and it's difficult for the eyes to adjust from light to dark.

4

You can see covered bridges on the following rides: Blue Ball, Intercourse, Lancaster County Covered Bridges, Quarryville, Thompsontown, and Loganton. On the third Sunday of August, the Lancaster Bicycle Club sponsors its Covered Bridge Metric Century. This is a noncompetitive, 100-kilometer ride that goes through seven covered bridges, and usually attracts more than 1,500 riders. Most of the ride goes through Amish farmlands, and the club provides food and sag wagons. If you'd like more information, call the club's hotline at 717–396–9299 for a recorded message.

Here are some facts on the covered bridges on the rides:

| Ride | Bridge Name | Length | Stream | Year Built |
|------|-------------|--------|--------|-----------|
| Atglen | Mercer's Mill | 85' | Octorara Creek | 1860 |
| Blue Ball | Weaver Mill | 88' | Conestoga River | 1879 |
| Intercourse | Leaman Place | 118' | Pequea Creek | 1894 |
| Lancaster Co* | Samuel Erb's | 80' | Hammer Creek | 1887 |
| Lancaster Co | Rosehill | 89' | Cocalico Creek | 1849 |
| Lancaster Co | Eberly's Mill | 99' | Conestoga River | 1846 |
| Lancaster Co | Pinetown | 133' | Conestoga River | 1867 |
| Lancaster Co | Hunsecker | 180' | Conestoga River | 1975** |
| Loganton | Logan's Mill | 63' | Big Fishing Creek | 1874 |
| Quarryville | Jackson's Mill | 142' | Octorara Creek | 1878 |
| Thompsontown | Lehman/Port Royal | 120' | Licking Creek | 1888 |

*Bridges on Lancaster County Covered Bridges ride are listed in order they appear on the ride.

**Hurricane Agnes washed away the original Hunsecker Bridge, built in 1843.

## Rail Trails

The decline of the railroad industry has been a boon to bike riders and hikers in Pennsylvania. Many abandoned railroad rights-of-way have become rail trails, and this edition contains six such trail rides: Downingtown, Valley Forge to Philadelphia, Montoursville, Jim Thorpe, Wellsboro, and New Freedom. These trails allow you

to ride with no thoughts of cars. Other rail trails are under development. For more information you can call the Pennsylvania Department of Conservation and Natural Resources at (717) 787–6674 or check their Web site at http://www.dcnr.state.pa.us.

## Pennsylvania's Topography and Roads

Few people with a casual knowledge of the state would associate mountains with Pennsylvania, but Pennsylvania *is* a mountain state. If you look at a map, you'll see the word *mountain* all over the place. The one exception is the southeast corner of the state. East and south of Harrisburg, it's comparatively flat, but it's still not like central Illinois. As a result, most of these rides take the rider over some hills. Because of the terrain, Pennsylvania's roads are rarely straight. They bend to follow a creek or to avoid a mountain.

To help you choose rides that are comfortable for you, here's the author's rating of the hilliest and the flattest rides:

*Hilliest:* Eagles Mere, Mt. Gretna/Mt. Hope
*Flattest:* Athens, Valley Forge to Philadelphia, Harvey's Lake, Downingtown, Washingtonville, Hershey, Bird-in-Hand, Wellsboro, New Freedom, Jim Thorpe, Montoursville.

> The advantage to riding a bike
> Is that as you head down the pike
> You see near and far
> Things you miss in a car
> It's a feeling that you're sure to like

The Globe Pequot Press assumes no liability for accidents happening to, or injuries sustained by, readers who engage in the activities described in this book.

# Atglen

| | |
|---:|:---|
| **Number of miles:** | 13.2 |
| **Approximate pedaling time:** | 1 hour, 15 minutes |
| **Terrain:** | Mostly flat, with one long climb |
| **Surface:** | Good |
| **Things to see:** | Small towns, covered bridge, Pennsylvania Scenic River System area |
| **Food:** | In Atglen and Christiana |
| **Facilities:** | In Atglen and Christiana |

This short ride provides a variety of beautiful sights as it takes you through two small towns, a covered bridge, a farming area, and a section of the Pennsylvania Scenic Rivers System along the Octorara Creek.

Atglen and Christiana are small towns on either side of the creek. Amish buggies are frequent sights in town and on the surrounding country roads. In Christiana, you'll see some beautiful old homes on tree-lined streets.

At 3.7 miles, you'll pass under an impressive stone railroad bridge. This was part of the Atglen–Susquehanna line, commonly known as the Low Grade Line. Built in the early years of the twentieth century, the Low Grade Line was an engineering marvel. It traveled 34 miles to the Susquehanna River with no road crossings. The railroad has abandoned the line and local groups are attempting to turn it into a hiking/biking trail.

The covered bridge at 5 miles is a nice place to pause and watch the water flow. Frequently, ducks and geese swim here, and many deer call the region home. The ride's one hard climb comes after the covered bridge.

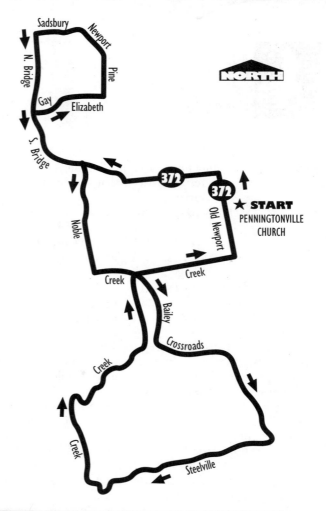

NORTH

Sadsbury

Newport

Pine

N. Bridge

Gay

Elizabeth

S. Bridge

372

372
★ START
PENNINGTONVILLE
CHURCH

Old Newport

Noble

Creek

Creek

Bailey

Crossroads

Creek

Creek

Steelville

**HOW to get there** From U.S. Route 30 at Gap in eastern Lancaster County, go south on Route 41. At the traffic light after the railroad bridge, go west on Route 372. Penningtonville Presbyterian Church is at the first intersection.

- Begin at Penningtonville Presbyterian Church, corner of Main (372 & Ridge).
- Go west on Route 372.
- Right on Gay Street at 1.7 miles.
- Left at arrow and under bridge at 1.8 miles.
- Right on Elizabeth Street at 2.1 miles.
- Left on Pine Street at 2.2 miles.
- Left on Newport at 2.4 miles.
- Left on Sadsbury at 2.5 miles.
- Left on North Bridge Street at 2.6 miles.
- Straight onto South Bridge Street at 3.0 miles.
- Right onto Noble Road (SR 2009) at 3.5 miles.
- Left on Creek Road at 4.4 miles.
- Bend to right—to covered bridge at 4.5 miles.
- Bear left on Bailey's Crossroads Road to covered bridge at 5.0 miles.
- Right at top of hill at 6.3 miles.
- Right on Steelville Road at 8.5 miles.
- Right on Creek Road at 8.6 miles.
- Creek turns right at 9.0 miles.
- Creek turns right at 11.7 miles.
- Right over concrete bridge and onto Creek Road at 12.0 miles.
- Left on Old Newport Pike at 12.9 miles.
- Finish at 13.2 miles.

**Note:** This ride does have two separate Creek Roads: one in Chester County and one in Lancaster County.

From 8.5 to 12 miles, you'll ride beside the Octorara Creek. This stretch is about as pretty a place as you'll find anywhere, and even on summer's hottest days the tall trees block out the sun and hold the temperature down.

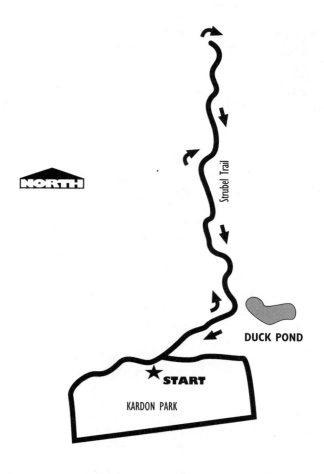

NORTH

Strubel Trail

DUCK POND

★ START

KARDON PARK

**HOW** to get there
Take Business Route 30 into downtown Downingtown. From the intersection of 282 and U.S. Route 30, go one block north on Green Street. Then go right on Pennsylvania Avenue. Kardon Park is on the left.

# Downingtown

| | |
|---:|:---|
| **Number of miles:** | 6.2 |
| **Approximate pedaling time:** | $^{1}/_{2}$ hour |
| **Terrain:** | Absolutely flat |
| **Surface:** | Fair |
| **Things to see:** | Duck pond, shaded trail |
| **Facilities:** | In park at beginning of trail |

Pennsylvania has only a few biking trails. The Strubel Biking/Hiking Trail is a nice one. It's short and isn't suitable for fast riding, but it's an excellent place for parents and children to ride together and for children to learn to ride.

The trail, which utilizes an abandoned railroad right-of-way, is flat. A single-speed bike will work quite well here. The Brandywine Creek runs beside the trail, and tall trees line most of the route.

Since the trail is used by both hikers and bikers, it's important to be courteous to pedestrians, who usually outnumber bikers. Frequently, parents walk or run while their small children ride alongside.

Downingtown is a small, quiet town located on the outer reaches of the Philadelphia metropolitan area. The trail begins at Kardon Park, where a small pond is home to many ducks.

**DIRECTIONS for the ride**

- The Strubel Trail begins in Kardon Park and runs north, along the Brandywine Creek, for 3.1 miles.

# Philadelphia

| | |
|---|---|
| **Number of miles:** | 12, 17, or 25 |
| **Approximate pedaling time:** | $\frac{1}{2}$ hour to 3 hours |
| **Terrain:** | Flat, unless you go looking for hills |
| **Surface:** | Good |
| **Things to see:** | Philadelphia Museum of Art, Liberty Bell, Independence Hall, Memorial Hall, Fairmount Park, Penn's Landing, Academy of Natural Sciences, Boathouse Row, Mann Music Center, and much more |
| **Food:** | Many places on ride |
| **Facilities:** | At Fairmount Park, Independence Hall, and many other places |
| **Options:** | Ride up the Manayunk Wall (5 miles); ride through Center City (8 miles) |

As the biggest city in the state and the "birthplace of liberty," Philadelphia offers many interesting attractions. It also has plenty of traffic; so much, in fact, that radio stations give traffic reports at midnight. Thus, this is more of a guide than a strictly planned ride. The best time to ride in Philadelphia is on a Sunday morning; next best is a Sunday afternoon.

Fairmount Park is a great place to ride. It's green—you'll even find raspberries and mulberries growing wild—and there are a lot of ducks and geese living here. If you stand on Kelly Drive and look across the river, you can almost imagine that you're in a wilderness. Trees and water are just about all that you can see.

The Philadelphia Museum of Art, where the ride begins, is the

Silverwood
Levering
Rector
Churchview
Main
Terrace
Shurs
Ridge
Falls Bridge
Calumet
Belmont
Manor
W. River
Kelly
Concourse
Montgomery
West River Drive
Sweetbriar
Cutoff
★ **START**
MUSEUM OF ART

NORTH

Ben Franklin Pkwy.
Arch St.
3rd
Market
Penn's
Landing
15th
5th
Chestnut
Pine

**HOW to get there** The ride starts at the Philadelphia Museum of Art. The museum is beside the Schuylkill River, close to the Schuylkill Expressway (Interstate 76, which runs east and west). Exit the expressway at Thirtieth Street and follow the signs. Coming from the north or south, take Interstate 95 to the Vine Street Expressway and go west. Look for signs for Ben Franklin Parkway, which ends at the museum.

**DIRECTIONS for the ride**

- Start at Philadelphia Museum of Art and go north on West River Drive.
- Left at Sweetbriar Cutoff at 1.5 miles.
- Right onto Concourse Drive at 1.6 miles.
- Through big arches and straight to Mann Music Center.
- Road turns into Belmont Manor.
- Left onto Montgomery Drive at 5.0 miles.
- Left onto West River Drive at 5.4 miles.
- Right onto Falls Bridge Road at 7.3 miles.
- Right onto Kelly Drive at 7.5 miles.
- Return to art museum at 12 miles.

## Manayunk Wall Option

- At end of bridge at 7.3 miles (Falls Bridge Road), straight onto Calumet Street.
- Left onto Ridge Avenue.
- Bear left onto Main Street.
- Right onto Levering Street.
- Right onto Silverwood Street.
- Left onto Rector Street.
- Straight onto Churchview Street.
- Right onto Terrace Street.
- Right onto Shurs Lane.
- Left onto Main Street.
- Right onto Kelly Drive back to art museum.

## Center City Ride Option

- From art museum, go east on Ben Franklin Parkway.
- Left onto Arch Street.
- Right onto Fifteenth Street.
- Left onto Pine Street.
- Left onto Fifth Street (Independence Park is at Chestnut and Fifth streets).
- Right onto Chestnut Street to Penn's Landing.
- West on Market Street.

- Right onto Third Street.
- Left onto Arch Street.
- Right onto Ben Franklin Parkway to art museum.

---

place where Rocky ran up the steps. It's home to collections ranging from Renaissance paintings to ancient Chinese works. The museum is right on the edge of Fairmount Park, and many local riders flock to this area. On Kelly Drive and West River Drive, there are paths for biking and running. These are in pretty good shape and let you ride without fighting the cars.

Begin at the art museum and head west on West River Drive. You'll be riding beside the Schuylkill River. At the Sweetbriar cutoff at 1.5 miles, turn left; then turn right at the stop sign. This will put you on Concourse Drive and take you through Fairmount Park. You'll pass Memorial Hall, which was built for the Centennial Exposition in 1876. Go straight ahead and you'll pass the Mann Music Center. This is home to summer concerts. The road changes names, but just follow it. Eventually, it will become Belmont Manor Road. You'll see many horticultural exhibits in the park. When you come to a T intersection at 5.0 miles, make a left and go downhill. This will take you back to West River Drive.

Go left on West River Drive for about 2 miles. You'll come to Falls Bridge Road and a green metal bridge across the river. When you reach the other side, you'll have two options. If you go right, you can go back to the museum. If you'd like to ride up the Manayunk Wall, go left on Ridge Avenue. The Manayunk Wall is the toughest hill of the CoreStates Classic, a 156-mile bike race for the pros that's held here in June. To get to the wall, stay on Ridge Avenue for about 1½ miles. You'll come to an intersection where Ridge goes to the right and Main Street to the left. Take Main Street and go to Levering Street. Make a right and you'll be on "The Wall." It's a good hill, though not the toughest in Pennsylvania.

Back on Kelly Drive, you'll come to Boathouse Row. This is home to many rowing clubs, and on most days you can see rowers out on the river. At night, the houses are all lit up and make a striking sight, especially from the other side of the river. The Philadelphia Distance Run, a half marathon that attracts some of running's big names, is held on Kelly Drive and West River Drive on the third Sunday in September. Other bike races and running races take place here throughout the year.

You'll then come back to the art museum. If you wish to ride to such attractions as the Liberty Bell and Independence Hall, go in front of the museum, around the circle, and pick up Ben Franklin Parkway. This will take you into Center City. If you do choose to ride into Center City, expect to do battle with cars and trucks. When you reach the end of the Parkway, you'll be forced onto Arch Street. Here, you'll see signs for Tourist Information. Stopping here can be a good idea. They can give you information on what's going on at the moment and help you to plot your course.

To get to the Liberty Bell, go right on Fifteenth Street and go down to Pine. Then go left on Pine and left on Fifth Street. The Liberty Bell and Independence Hall are in the area around Fifth and Chestnut. (If you'd like to see Veterans' Stadium, home of the Phillies and Eagles, turn right from Pine onto Broad Street. Broad Street would be Fourteenth Street if it were numbered. The stadium is about 3 miles to the south.)

To get to Penn's Landing, the waterfront area along the Delaware River, return here and head east on Chestnut Street. Go as far east as you can. When you reach the river, you'll find shops, a museum, ships, and eating establishments.

To return, take the Market Street overpass across Interstate 95. Go to Third Street and go right. Then go left on Arch Street. This will take you through Chinatown and back to the Ben Franklin Parkway, which will take you back to the art museum.

If traffic doesn't bother you, Philadelphia's a great place to ride. If you don't care for traffic, it's still a good ride if you time it properly.

# Valley Forge

| | |
|---:|:---|
| **Number of miles:** | 6 |
| **Approximate pedaling time:** | 1 hour |
| **Terrain:** | Moderately hilly |
| **Surface:** | Very good |
| **Things to see:** | Valley Forge National Historical Park |
| **Food:** | Snack bar on grounds |
| **Facilities:** | At visitors center and several places throughout park |

Valley Forge is one of the names forever associated with the American Revolution. It was here that George Washington and 12,000 troops staged a six-month encampment from December 1777 to June 1778. During that time they kept the British army holed up in Philadelphia. Two thousand American troops died from disease, lack of supplies, and the severe winter. Still, during those hard times, the American army was reorganized. When they broke camp, they were a highly trained and very efficient unit. In a very real sense, the events that took place at Valley Forge allowed the colonists to win the Revolutionary War.

Today Valley Forge Park is a peaceful oasis close to the sprawl of Philadelphia. Inside the park, all is serene. Joggers and bikers are everywhere, and the twentieth century's hectic pace doesn't intrude on the green fields.

The park has a trail for biking and hiking. You can also rent bikes here. Begin at the visitors center and the trail will take you to all of the important sites. The huts in which the soldiers lived are memorable; *primitive* is too kind a word for them. They're log cabins with single wooden slats that served as beds. Life was not terribly comfort-

**21**

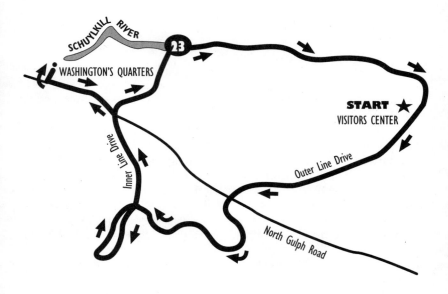

SCHUYLKILL RIVER

**23**

WASHINGTON'S QUARTERS

**START** ★
VISITORS CENTER

Inner Line Drive

Outer Line Drive

North Gulph Road

**HOW**
to get
there

Valley Forge is just northwest of
Philadelphia. Take the Pennsylvania Turnpike
to the Valley Forge exit (Exit 24). Take Route
422 west and follow the signs to the park. The
visitors center is on the right as you enter the park.

**DIREC-TIONS for the ride**

- Begin at the visitors center.
- Go right, picking up bike/hike path along Outer Line Drive.
- Follow the bike path, in a roughly clockwise direction, through the park.
- To reach Washington's Headquarters, leave the bike path at about 4 miles and go left on North Gulph Road.
- Take second right (Inner Line Drive).
- Return to bike path and follow it back to visitors center.

able for the soldiers of the Revolution. The generals, of course, had more comfortable quarters. They used their rank to take over several local farmhouses.

If you come in June or July, you'll find wild raspberries growing in profusion along the roadsides. You can pick a lot and have a meal on the park picnic grounds.

This ride is short but very pleasant. The park is popular with local riders. It gives them an opportunity to get away from the heavy traffic on the roads outside the park. Despite the ride's shortness, you'll want to allow plenty of time to stop and play tourist.

# **5** Valley Forge To Philadelphia

| | |
|---:|:---|
| Number of miles: | 44 |
| Approximate pedaling time: | 4 hours |
| Terrain: | Flat! |
| Surface: | Good and bad |
| Things to see: | Valley Forge, Schuylkill River, Main Street in Manayunk, Fairmount Park, Boathouse Row, Art Museum |
| Food: | In Philadelphia |
| Facilities: | Many places along route |

You can ride from Valley Forge to Philadelphia with only minimal interference from cars. The Schuylkill River Trail combines the Valley Forge Bikeway, the Manayunk Canal Towpath, and bike paths in Fairmount Park, along with about 1½ miles of roads, to make a beautiful and tranquil ride through one of the country's most congested regions.

This is a place for a pleasant ride, but not necessarily a fast one. The trail enjoys heavy use, so expect to share it with many other bicyclists, as well as walkers, runners, and rollerbladers.

The bikeway goes through one of the most heavily industrialized areas in the country. Many factories, working and abandoned, line the course, but in most areas trees actually block the view of the river. Early in the ride, you'll pass through the boroughs of Norristown and Conshohocken. Be careful at the street crossings. Frequently, bikers must stop for cars.

When the paved portion of the bikeway ends, you'll pick up the Manayunk Canal Towpath. This is a fairly rough surface, so strong tires are a necessity. Road bikes will work, but be cautious. The gravel portion of the ride is about 2 miles long.

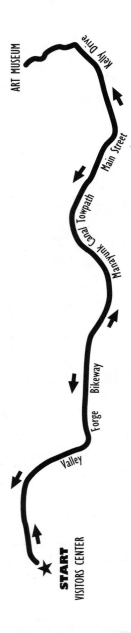

ART MUSEUM

Kelly Drive

Main Street

Manayunk (Canal Towpath)

Bikeway

Forge

Valley

**START**
VISITORS CENTER

**HOW** to get there

Follow the Pennsylvania Turnpike to the Valley Forge exit and follow the signs to the visitors center at Valley Forge National Historical Park. From there, follow signs for the Schuylkill River Trail.

- Begin at visitors center at Valley Forge Park and look for signs for Schuylkill River Trail.
- Go east on trail and follow signs.
- At Shawmont, 13.5 miles, trail becomes gravel to Manayunk.
- When trail ends in Manayunk, go left to Main Street and continue east.
- Follow sign to Kelly Drive. On Kelly Drive, bike path reappears.
- Follow bike path to art museum and reverse course.

When the towpath ends, you'll be on Main Street in Manayunk. This has become an upscale shopping region with nice restaurants and trendy shops. Still, bikes are common, and you'll feel quite comfortable in most restaurants in your biking clothes.

For about 1½ miles, you'll be on Main Street. This is the only section where you'll have to ride on roads. As soon as you reach Kelly Drive, you'll find a bike path. This path takes you along the Schuylkill to the art museum. Along the way, you'll pass lots of other bikers, runners, and so on. You'll also see rowers on the river and pass Boathouse Row, the area where the rowing clubs in Philadelphia keep their boats. The art museum gained added fame in the movie *Rocky*, and you'll probably see someone running up the steps whenever you're there.

*A hint:* The winds in Pennsylvania usually blow from west to east. Here, that means that the wind will be at your back when you begin this ride, and in your face when you return. Beginning at the art museum and riding to Valley Forge will usually put the wind at your back for the second half of the ride.

# French Creek

| | |
|---|---|
| **Number of miles:** | 19 or more. Exact distance will depend on riding done in French Creek Park. Distance between park and Daniel Boone Homestead is 9.5 miles. |
| **Approximate pedaling time:** | 2½ hours |
| **Terrain:** | Hilly |
| **Surface:** | Mostly good; rough in French Creek Park |
| **Things to see:** | Daniel Boone Homestead, French Creek State Park |
| **Food:** | At French Creek State Park |
| **Facilities:** | At Boone Homestead and French Creek Park |

This ride will take you over the back roads of eastern Berks County, through farmland and woodlands. Traffic is light and much of the route is shaded, so it's good for a hot day.

Daniel Boone was one of the great American frontiersmen. The Daniel Boone Homestead is maintained to show how Boone lived when he wasn't off exploring the wilds of the new nation. It also shows how the early English and German settlers in the area lived. On the grounds are Boone's house, a blacksmith shop, a barn, a sawmill, a visitors center, trails, and a picnic area.

When you leave the homestead, you'll pass through farm country for several miles. There are several horse farms, and it's not uncommon to see people riding horses down the road. After you cross Route 422, the farms decrease and the land becomes wooded. You'll ride through the very small town of Monocacy. On Shed Road you'll go up an extremely long hill. Fortunately, it's not extremely steep.

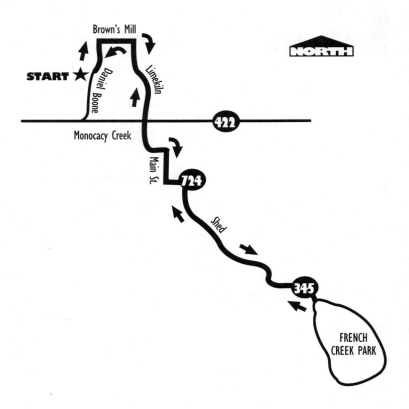

START ★

Brown's Mill

NORTH

Daniel Boone

Limekiln

422

Monocacy Creek

Main St.

724

Shed

345

FRENCH CREEK PARK

**HOW to get there** Take U.S. Route 422 east from Reading. Follow the signs to the Daniel Boone Homestead, which lies on Daniel Boone Road, just north of U.S. Route 422.

**DIREC-TIONS** for the ride

- Begin at visitors center at Daniel Boone Homestead and ride toward the entrance.
- Left on Daniel Boone Road at the entrance.
- Right on Brown's Mill Road at 1.5 miles.
- Right on Limekiln Road at 2.2 miles.
- Cross U.S. 422 at 4.4 miles onto Monocacy Creek Road.
- Right onto Main Street at 5.3 miles.
- Left onto Route 724 at 6.0 miles.
- Right onto Shed Road at 6.1 miles.
- Shed Road turns left at 6.6 miles.
- Left on Route 345 at 9.2 miles.
- Right into French Creek State Park at 9.4 miles.

## Reverse

- Leave French Creek State Park and go left on Route 345.
- Right on Shed Road at 0.2 mile.
- Shed Road turns right at 2.8 miles
- Left onto Route 724 at 3.3 miles.
- Right onto Main Street (no sign) at 3.4 miles.
- Left onto Monocacy Creek Road at 4.1 miles.
- Cross 422 onto Limekiln Road at 4.9 miles.
- Left onto Brown's Mill Road at 7.1 miles.
- Left onto Daniel Boone Road at 7.9 miles.
- Right into Daniel Boone Homestead at 8.7 miles.

Shed Road ends right at the entrance to French Creek State Park. Here you'll find swimming, boat rentals, trails, and food. You'll also see signs for Hopewell Furnace National Historic Site. The furnace, which operated from 1771 until 1883, produced pig iron, hollowware, stoves, and many other items. Many of the structures have been restored, and there are daily demonstrations of metal making during the summer. A visitors center has displays and examples of the tools used here and the pieces cast in the furnace.

The best part of the ride back is that you can go down the hill that you had to go up before.

# Trexlertown

| | |
|---:|:---|
| **Number of miles:** | 21 |
| **Approximate pedaling time:** | 1¾ hours |
| **Terrain:** | Hilly |
| **Surface:** | Good |
| **Things to see:** | Bike races at Lehigh County Velodrome; Rodale Research Center |
| **Food:** | Best to bring your own |
| **Facilities:** | At Velodrome and Research Center |

This is a scenic, low-traffic, out-and-back ride that will give you an opportunity to ride in a way that you've probably never experienced before. You'll also have an opportunity to see food produced in a very unusual way.

Trexlertown is just south of Allentown. It is the home of the Lehigh County Velodrome, one of just a few bike-racing tracks in the United States. On Tuesday and Friday nights throughout the summer, riders from beginners to world champions race around the concrete oval. Track racing is not at all like road racing. The bikes have only one gear and no brakes. The riders spend much of their time jockeying for position. Then they sprint madly to the finish. The margin of victory is often less than a wheel.

If you'd like to give track riding a try, you're welcome to do so. The Velodrome is open to the public most of the time. Generally, the pros work out in the morning and evening; afternoons are best for amateurs. But be careful when you get on the track. It's steeply banked, and it's impossible if it's wet. For a racing schedule, call the Velodrome at (215) 965–6930.

When you leave the Velodrome, you'll travel for 10.5 miles through beautiful farmland over the hills of Lehigh and Berks coun-

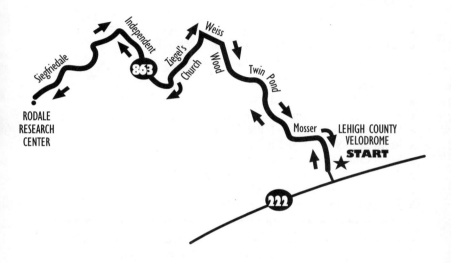

**HOW to get there** Trexlertown is on U.S. Route 222, south of Allentown and north of Reading. The ride begins at the Velodrome, which is on 222, just south of the traffic light. Coming from the north, bear right on Mosser Road at a Mobil station. From the south, make a left on Mosser just after you pass Cycle Sports, the local bike shop.

**DIREC-TIONS for the ride**

- Leave Velodrome parking lot and go right on Mosser Road.
- Right onto Twin Pond Road at 1.4 miles.
- Right onto Wood Lane at 3.7 miles.
- Left onto Weiss Road at 4.4 miles.
- Left onto Ziegel's Church Road at 4.6 miles.
- Right onto Independent Road (Route 863 north) at 5.7 miles.
- Left onto Siegfriedale Road at 8.2 miles.
- Rodale Research Center at 10.5 miles.

## Reverse

- Head back on Siegfriedale Road.
- Right on Independent Road (Route 863 south) at 2.1 miles.
- Left onto Ziegel's Church Road at 4.7 miles.
- Right onto Weiss Road at 5.7 miles.
- Right onto Wood Lane at 5.9 miles.
- Left onto Twin Pond Road at 6.6 miles.
- Left onto Mosser Road at 8.9 miles.
- Return to Velodrome at 10.5 miles.

ties. On Siegfriedale Road you will come to a little red schoolhouse. This is the visitors center and bookstore for the Rodale Research Center. The Rodale family publishes such magazines as *Prevention* and *Bicycling* in nearby Emmaus. On this research farm, they're exploring ways to produce foods without using harmful chemicals. If you take a tour of this farm, you'll see the food that looks perfect without the benefit of pesticides or herbicides. The apples shine as brilliantly as any sprayed with Alar.

One of the most interesting parts of the Rodale farm is the amaranth project. Amaranth is a hardy annual plant that's native to the Americas. It's drought resistant and high in protein, and it was an important food crop for the Aztecs. When amaranth is ripe, usually in August, the heads turn flaming red.

The people who work here are seriously involved in what they're doing, and they are happy to discuss their work.

# Harrisburg

| | |
|---|---|
| **Number of miles:** | 15.5 |
| **Approximate pedaling time:** | 1½ hours |
| **Terrain:** | Flat |
| **Surface:** | Good |
| **Things to see:** | State Capitol, State Museum, Farm Show, Museum of Scientific Discovery, Harrisburg Senators baseball team, Harrisburg Marathon, Dauphin County Historical Society |
| **Food:** | All along the route |
| **Facilities:** | All along the route |

Pennsylvania's capital city has many sights to see and offers a surprisingly nice city ride. Of course, it's best not to ride during morning or evening rush hour.

The first few miles are through an industrial area; although there's not a lot of traffic here, most of it is trucks. Still, it's a place favored by local bikers. After you leave the industrial area, you'll move onto Sixth Street, a broad boulevard, and then follow a designated bike route for a few miles. Front Street is a good place to try out your speed. It's straight and flat. It's best, however, not to exceed the posted speed limits. Below Front Street, at the water's edge, is a trail that's good for walking, running, and biking—except during floods.

The river is the Susquehanna. It's too shallow and rocky for shipping but it is wide. Upstream there are long stretches without a bridge. City Island, in the middle of the river, offers many recreational opportunities. The Harrisburg Senators minor league baseball team plays here, and the Harrisburg Marathon, held in November, finishes here.

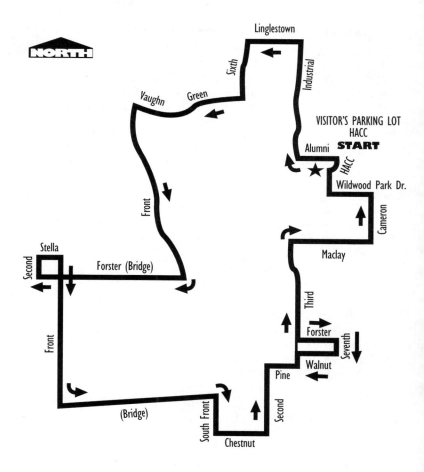

NORTH

Linglestown

Sixth

Industrial

Green

Vaughn

VISITOR'S PARKING LOT
HACC
START

Alumni

HACC

Front

Wildwood Park Dr.

Cameron

Maclay

Stella

Second

Forster (Bridge)

Front

Third

Forster

Seventh

Walnut

Pine

Front

(Bridge)

South Front

Second

Chestnut

**HOW to get there** Harrisburg is accessible via the Pennsylvania Turnpike, Interstate 83, U.S. Route 322, and U.S. Route 22. The ride begins at Harrisburg Area Community College (HACC) on Cameron Street, U.S. Route 22, just north of the farm show. An exit from Interstate 81 is right there.

**DIRECTIONS for the ride**

- Leave the HACC visitors parking lot and go left on Alumni Drive.
- Right onto Industrial Road at 0.1 mile.
- Left onto Linglestown Road at 2.5 miles.
- Left onto Sixth Street (sign for bike route).
- Right onto Green Street at 3.8 miles.
- Right onto Vaughn Street at 4.7 miles.
- Left onto Front Street at 4.9 miles.
- Right onto Forster Street at 7.6 miles.
- Cross the Susquehanna River.
- Right onto Second Street at 8.4 miles.
- Right onto Stella Avenue at 8.5 miles.
- Right onto Front Street (U.S. Routes 11 and 15) at 8.6 miles.
- Left onto bridge at 9.8 miles (sign: HARRISBURG 1).
- Right onto South Front Street at 10.6 miles.
- Left onto Chestnut Street at 10.7 miles.
- Left onto Second Street at 10.8 miles.
- Right onto Pine Street at 11.2 miles.
- Left onto Third Street at 11.3 miles.
- Right onto Forster Street at 11.4 miles.
- Right onto Seventh Street at 11.7 miles.
- Right onto Walnut Street at 12.1 miles.
- Right onto Third Street at 12.3 miles.
- Right onto Maclay Street at 13.7 miles.
- Left onto Cameron Street (U.S. Route 22) at 14.6 miles (farm show).
- Right onto Wildwood Park Drive at 15.0 miles.
- Left onto HACC Drive at 15.2 miles.
- Left onto Alumni Drive at 15.5 miles.

Back on solid ground, you'll see the State Capitol, an impressive edifice where Pennsylvania's legislators meet. Inside Strawberry Square, a shopping complex at Third and Walnut, is the Museum of Scientific Discovery. This is a hands-on science center with some fascinating displays. The State Museum, on Third between North and Forster, details the history of geology, science, industry, the military, and much more in Pennsylvania.

Near the end of the ride, on Cameron Street, is the State Farm Show Building. The Farm Show is held every January, and snow always falls during Farm Show week. Other events such as Auto Shows and Home Builders Shows are also held here. There's even a Horse Show in October. In years past many basketball games were played here, but the dusty arena never won great favor with fans or players.

**Hershey**

| | |
|---:|:---|
| **Number of miles:** | 10 |
| **Approximate pedaling time:** | 1¹/₂ hours |
| **Terrain:** | Rolling to flat |
| **Surface:** | Good |
| **Things to see:** | Hershey Park, Chocolate World, |
| | Founder's Hall, Hershey Park Arena |
| **Food:** | Everywhere |
| **Facilities:** | Numerous |

The small town of Hershey has a big reputation for supplying the world with chocolate and with fun. The Hershey Bar is perhaps the most famous piece of candy in the world, and Hershey Park is Pennsylvania's version of Disneyland. This is a town where people come to enjoy themselves and to eat. The ride takes you to the major attractions in town. The street lights are shaped like Hershey Kisses, and the streets have names such as Chocolate Avenue and Cocoa Avenue. The prevailing aroma is that of chocolate.

The ride begins at the Hershey Park Visitors Center and takes you on a jaunt around town. Hershey is a developed area, but most of it remains green; in fact, there are still farms right in town. The reason is the Milton Hershey School. This school, founded by the man behind the chocolate company, cares for and educates children whose parents are unable to do so. It has some of the most impressive grounds and athletic facilities of any school anywhere.

On the school grounds is Founder's Hall, a monument to Milton and Catherine Hershey. It has a visitors center, a Heritage room, a banquet hall, and an auditorium. Tours are available.

Hershey Park offers more than forty rides and food of almost all

**40**

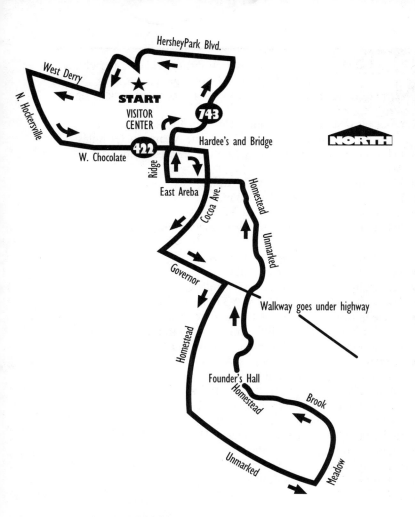

HersheyPark Blvd.

West Derry

N. Hockersville

START

VISITOR
CENTER

743

Hardee's and Bridge

422

W. Chocolate

Ridge

East Areba

Cocoa Ave.

Homestead

Unmarked

Governor

Walkway goes under highway

Homestead

Founder's Hall

Homestead

Brook

Unmarked

Meadow

NORTH

**HOW**
to get
there

Hershey is about 10 miles east of
Harrisburg. U.S. Routes 322 and
422 and Routes 743 and 39 go
through town. The ride starts at the
visitors center on U.S. Route 743.

**DIRECTIONS for the ride**

- From HersheyPark Visitors Center, go right; follow EXIT signs. At stop sign, go left.
- Bear right onto West Derry Road at YIELD sign at 0.3 mile.
- Left on North Hockersville Road at 0.6 mile.
- Left on West Chocolate Avenue at 1.1 miles.
- Left onto main portion of U.S. Route 422 (West Chocolate Avenue) at 1.4 miles.
- Right onto Cocoa Avenue at 2.0 miles.
- Left onto Governor Road at 2.6 miles.
- Right onto Homestead Lane at 3.2 miles.
- Left at dead end (sign in middle of road) at 4.0 miles. Road is unmarked.
- Left onto Meadow Lane at 4.6 miles.
- Left onto Brook Drive at 5.2 miles.
- Bear right onto Homestead at 5.9 miles.
- Bear right to Founder's Hall at 6.3 miles.
- Circle in front of Founder's Hall and head back out.
- Right at bottom of little hill, onto walking trail at 6.5 miles.
- Left at pond, onto walkway that runs under highway.
- Right at first road after underpass.
- Left at stop sign at 7.2 miles.
- Right back onto Homestead at 7.9 miles.
- Left onto East Areba Avenue at 8.1 miles.
- Right onto Ridge Avenue at 8.5 miles.
- Right and quick left under bridge at Hardee's at 8.7 miles.
- Right at stop sign after bridge.
- Left onto Route 743 at 9.0 miles.
- Left onto HersheyPark Boulevard at 9.5 miles.
- Left to visitors center at 10 miles.

known varieties. It has theaters with live entertainment, and from the Kissing Tower you can get a great view of the surrounding valley. Chocolate World will show you just how cacao beans and milk join forces to produce milk chocolate. HersheyPark Arena is home to the Hershey Bears minor league hockey team, and it hosts concerts and events such as professional wrestling. It was in this building that Wilt Chamberlain scored 100 points in a game against New York in 1962.

# Marietta

| | |
|---:|:---|
| **Number of miles:** | 14.7 |
| **Approximate pedaling time:** | 1½ hours |
| **Terrain:** | Rolling |
| **Surface:** | Good |
| **Things to see:** | Small towns and big houses, Cameron Estate Inn |
| **Food:** | Stores and restaurants in Marietta and Maytown |
| **Facilities:** | At park on East High Street in Maytown |

A ride around Marietta will take you through several small towns, over country roads, and past plenty of farms. And this ride doesn't have any really steep hills; it's either gently rolling or flat.

In Marietta, as you ride down Market Street, you'll see a lot of magnificent homes. They're big and architecturally intriguing. Several even have stained-glass windows. In the center of town are the kinds of businesses that you'd expect to find in a small town: grocery stores, restaurants, and hardware stores.

As you leave Marietta, you go directly from town to the country. There really aren't any outskirts of this town. You'll ride past several farms, then into Maytown. This is a picturesque metropolis of perhaps a thousand. It has a beautiful little square with trees in the middle of the intersection. There are several businesses and a restaurant on the square.

Just east of the Maytown square, on East High Street, is a park where you can stop to refresh yourself. A few miles later, on Donegal Springs Road, you'll see the Donegal Witness Church and the remains

**44**

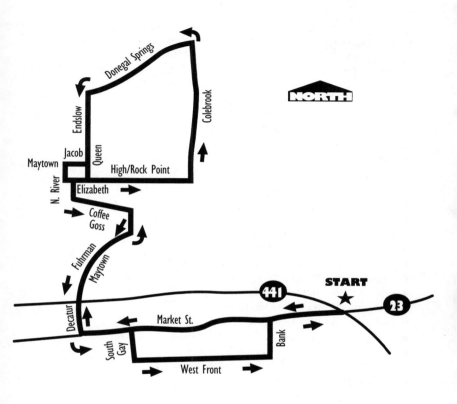

NORTH

Donegal Springs

Endslow

Jacob

Maytown

Queen

Colebrook

High/Rock Point

N. River

Elizabeth

Coffee

Goss

Fuhrman

Maytown

Decatur

441

START

23

Market St.

Bank

South Gay

West Front

**HOW to get there**    Marietta lies at the intersection of Routes 23, 441, and 743, about 3 miles north of Columbia and U.S. Route 30. From Route 30, exit at 441 and go north. You can park on West Market Street, near the intersection of 23 and 441.

**DIRECTIONS for the ride**

- Go west on Market Street.
- Right onto Decatur Street at 1.8 miles.
- Cross Route 441 onto Maytown Road at 2.1 miles.
- Right onto Fuhrman Road at 2.4 miles.
- Left onto Coffee Goss Road at 2.9 miles.
- Bear right at church at 3.9 miles.
- Right onto Elizabeth Street at 4.0 miles.
- Left onto Queen Street at 4.1 miles.
- Left onto Jacob Street at 4.3 miles.
- Left onto North River Road at 4.4 miles.
- Left onto East High Street at 4.5 miles (town square).
- High Street becomes Rock Point Road.
- Left onto Colebrook Road at 6.2 miles.
- Left onto Donegal Springs Road at 7.9 miles.
- Left onto Endslow Road at 9.1 miles.
- Right onto Elizabeth Street at 10.5 miles.
- Left onto Coffee Goss Road at 10.6 miles.
- Right onto Fuhrman Road at 11.1 miles.
- Left onto Maytown Road at 12.1 miles.
- Cross Route 441 onto Decatur Street at 12.5 miles.
- Left onto Market Street at 12.7 miles.
- Right onto South Gay Street at 13.3 miles.
- Left onto West Front Street at 13.4 miles.
- Left at bank at 14.3 miles (no street sign).
- Right onto Market Street at 14.4 miles.
- Finish at 14.7 miles.

of the Donegal Witness Tree. This tree was around for hundreds of years, and a plaque commemorates it. Next door to the Donegal Witness Church is the Cameron Estate Inn, a restored inn from the early 1800s. It now has guest rooms and a restaurant. Just past here is an airport; watch out for low-flying aircraft. When you return to Marietta, you'll turn onto Front Street. From this thoroughfare you can walk down to the Susquehanna River. There are several paved paths that cross the Conrail tracks and lead to the water. On Front Street you'll see antiques shops as well as neighborhood taverns. It's an interesting mix.

# Fredericksburg

| | |
|---:|:---|
| **Number of miles:** | 11.7 |
| **Approximate pedaling time:** | 1 hour |
| **Terrain:** | Rolling |
| **Surface:** | Good |
| **Things to see:** | Small town, farms, mountains |
| **Food:** | In Fredericksburg |
| **Facilities:** | In Fredericksburg |

Fredericksburg is a small town that lies at the base of a mountain, and the region around it is a rich agricultural area that's excellent for biking. The scenery is nice and the traffic is light. This ride takes you through Fredericksburg and farm areas, but does not include any mountain climbing.

Most of this ride will put you on lightly traveled country roads through cornfields and wooded areas. For much of the ride you'll be on Mountain Road, but Mountain Road isn't mountainous. Actually, it runs along the base of the mountain, and it's pretty flat.

Fredericksburg itself is a major agribusiness center. In addition to the farms that surround the town, several large agricultural businesses operate here. The main street is wide, with an old hotel, restaurants, and stores. Fredericksburg is generally a placid place, but on the third Saturday in September it gets a little wild with the Hinkle Fest, a country fair with rides, food, and a 5 km foot race.

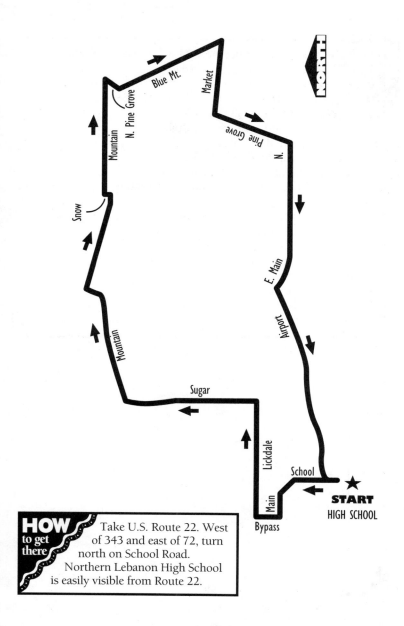

NORTH

Blue Mt.

N. Pine Grove

Mountain

Market

Pine Grove

N.

Snow

E. Main

Mountain

Airport

Sugar

Lickdale

School

Main

START
HIGH SCHOOL

Bypass

**HOW** to get there
Take U.S. Route 22. West of 343 and east of 72, turn north on School Road. Northern Lebanon High School is easily visible from Route 22.

**DIRECTIONS for the ride**

- Begin at Northern Lebanon High School.
- North on School Road.
- Bear left at 0.5 mile.
- Left on Main Street at 0.7 mile.
- Right on Bypass at 0.9 mile.
- Right on Lickdale Road at 1.1 miles.
- Left on Sugar Road at 2.2 miles.
- Right on Mountain Road at 4.0 miles.
- Left on Mountain at intersection at 5.1 miles.
- Left on Snow Road at 6.0 miles and immediately go right on Mountain.
- Right on Pine Grove Street at 7.4 miles.
- Left on Blue Mountain Drive at 7.7 miles.
- Right on Market Drive at 8.7 miles.
- Left on North Pine Grove Street at 9.6 miles.
- Right on East Main Street at 10.5 miles.
- Left on Airport Drive at 10.6 miles.
- Left on School Road at 1.5 miles.
- Finish at 11.7 miles.

# Myerstown

| | |
|---|---|
| **Number of miles:** | 16.3 |
| **Approximate pedaling time:** | 1½ hours |
| **Terrain:** | Rolling, no difficult hills |
| **Surface:** | Good |
| **Things to see:** | Farms, trains, small towns |
| **Food:** | In Myerstown and Richland |
| **Facilities:** | In Myerstown and Richland |

The major industry in Myerstown is Bayer Aspirin but this ride won't give you any headaches. Myerstown is a small town in a rich agricultural region, and biking here will take you over country roads and through two small towns.

Myerstown Borough park is a placid place where ducks swim in the creek and the pond. The surrounding countryside is a fine place to spin your wheels on a leisurely ride, and if you like to watch trains, you'll have many opportunities to see them on a busy freight line that runs through the valley.

This ride isn't completely flat, but it doesn't have any especially difficult hills, and it has some long, flat stretches. The farms in the region are generally small, and Amish families own many of them. In summer roadside stands offer the harvest directly to buyers.

Halfway through the ride you'll return to Myerstown. You can either end the ride there or continue. If you continue, you'll go through downtown Myerstown where you can dine and shop.

The most scenic part of the ride comes on Bollinger and Hickory roads where the road runs through a wooded area beside a creek. Then it's back into farmlands and into the small town of Richland where you'll find a store and the railroad tracks. If you do see a train, it will probably be a long one. This is a major

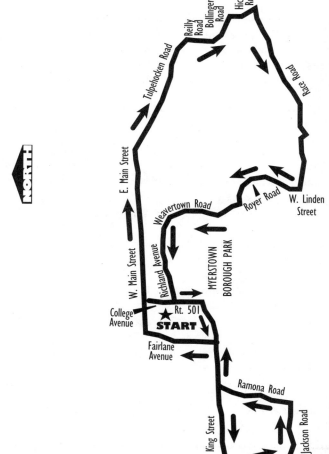

NORTH

Hickory Road

Bollinger Road

Reilly Road

Tulpehocken Road

Race Road

E. Main Street

W. Linden Street

Weavertown Road

Royer Road

W. Main Street

Richland Avenue

MYERSTOWN BOROUGH PARK

College Avenue

★ Rt. 501
START

Fairlane Avenue

Ramona Road

King Street

Jackson Road

Prescott Road

**HOW** to get there  Myerstown lies at the intersection of U.S. Route 422 and PA Route 501 in southeastern Pennsylvania. The ride begins at Myerstown Borough Park, which is on 501, about 3/4 mile south of 422.

**DIREC-TIONS for the ride**

- From the southern parking area in the park, go south on 501.
- Right on King Street at 0.3 mile.
- Left on Prescott Road (four-way stop) at 3.0 miles.
- Left on Jackson Road at 3.5 miles.
- Left on Ramona Road at 4.6 miles.
- Right on King Street at 5.4 miles.
- Left on Fairlane Avenue at 6.0 miles.
- Right on West Main Street at 6.8 miles.
- Right on College Avenue (501) at 7.8 miles to finish at 8.3 miles.

## To continue the ride

- Continue straight from West Main Street to East Main Street at 7.8 miles.
- Bear right on Tulpehocken Road at 9.1 miles.
- Right on Reilly Road at 10.4 miles.
- Left on Bollinger Road at 10.6 miles.
- Right on Hickory Road at stop sign at 11.0 miles.
- Right on Race Road at 11.9 miles.
- Store at 12.7 miles.
- Straight across tracks at 12.7 miles.
- Right on West Linden Avenue at 13.1 miles.
- Right on Royer Road at 13.5 miles.
- Right on Weavertown Road at 14.9 miles.
- Weavertown becomes Richland Avenue.
- Right on College Avenue at 16.2 miles.
- Finish at 16.3 miles.

east/west Conrail line, and trains rumble across these tracks all day and night. If you stop for lunch in Richland, you may be able to finish your meal in the time it takes a train to pass. From Richland it's an easy ride over scenic roads back to the park in Myerstown.

# New Freedom–York County Heritage Rail Trail

| | |
|---:|:---|
| **Number of miles:** | 9.5 each way |
| **Approximate pedaling time:** | 2 hours |
| **Terrain:** | Almost flat |
| **Surface:** | Good |
| **Things to see:** | Northern Central Railroad, emu farm, small towns |
| **Food:** | In New Freedom, Railroad, and Glen Rock |
| **Facilities:** | At ends of trail and in Glen Rock. A bike shop is beside the trail in New Freedom, and the owners put a jug of water outside on hot days. |

The York County Heritage Rail Trail offers a scenic ride through the woods, farms, and small towns of southern York County. This trail shares the corridor with an active rail line, so you may see—and hear—a train. It's a slow train, though, and bikes can go faster than it does. The trail runs beside the tracks of The Northern Central Railway, a tourist/dinner train that operates primarily on weekends over a historic railroad right-of-way. For information on the dinner trains, call 800–94–TRAIN. Abraham Lincoln traveled along this route on his way to deliver the Gettsburg Address, and freight trains used it until Hurricane Agnes severely damaged the line in 1972.

Today the York Country Heritage Rail Trail is a flat recreational corridor through a rather hilly area. Along the trail you'll see an

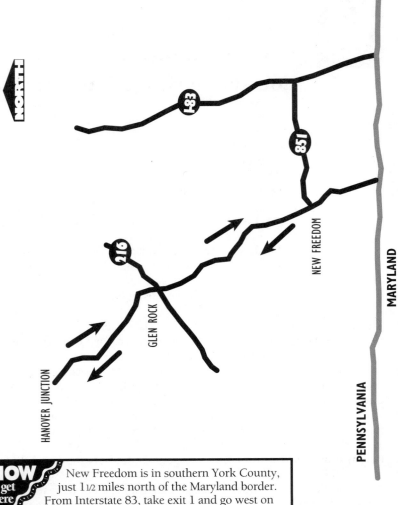

NORTH

I-83

851

216

HANOVER JUNCTION

GLEN ROCK

NEW FREEDOM

PENNSYLVANIA

MARYLAND

**HOW to get there** New Freedom is in southern York County, just 1½ miles north of the Maryland border. From Interstate 83, take exit 1 and go west on Route 851 for 4 miles to New Freedom. In New Freedom turn left on Franklin Street. A parking area for the trail is a block ahead, adjacent to the Northern Central Railway.

**DIRECTIONS for the ride**

- When you're in New Freedom, it can be hard to figure out which way is north and which is south. The best tip is to go toward the train cars. When you do that, you'll be heading north.

emu farm and several small towns where you can stop for supplies. Glen Rock is the biggest settlement, and the trail goes straight through the center of town, past restaurants and stores.

On weekends the trail fills with runners, walkers, and bikers, so if you're interested in cruising, it's best to visit on a weekday. The highlight of the trail is the opportunity to ride without having to think about cars, except at road crossings. The scenery is excellent, and on hot days the trees keep much of the trail pleasantly shaded.

New Freedom is the highest point on the trail, and the grade is noticeable in spots. If you do tire, however, you can sit and rest on one of the many benches along the way.

From New Freedom you can ride in either direction. The Maryland/Pennsylvania border is just 1½ miles to the south, and the trail continues for about 23 miles in Maryland, so if you ride the entire route, you'll have a nice 68-mile-long ride.

# Bird-In-Hand

| | |
|---:|:---|
| **Number of miles:** | 17 |
| **Approximate pedaling time:** | 1½ hours |
| **Terrain:** | Flat |
| **Surface:** | Fair; be careful of ruts worn by horses |
| **Things to see:** | Bird-In-Hand Farmers Market, Mascot Roller Mill, Miller's Store, Amish farmlands |
| **Food:** | Farmer's market, Kauffman's Store, Millers Store, roadside produce stands |
| **Facilities:** | At Farmers Market, outhouses at one-room schools on course |

Bird-In-Hand is in the heart of Pennsylvania Dutch country. The area nearby is one of the world's most fertile agricultural regions, and it's also a great place for biking. The back roads are numerous, and the traffic on them is light. In fact, much of the traffic consists of Amish horses and buggies, not cars.

Because the Amish are an agrarian society, most of the area's attractions center on food. At the Bird-In-Hand Farmers Market, where the ride begins, you can find many familiar favorites and perhaps some local delicacies that aren't found everywhere else. In summer and fall, local produce is abundant.

As you begin the ride, you immediately enter farm country. You'll probably see some farmers working their fields with teams of draft horses. The Amish don't use modern equipment, but their farms are tremendously productive. Most of these farms are relatively small, and every member of the family pitches in.

On many of the farms, you'll see signs advertising nonfood items

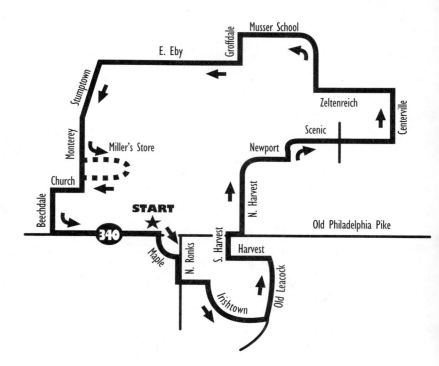

North

Musser School
Groffdale
E. Eby
Zeltenreich
Centerville
Stumptown
Scenic
Newport
Monterey
Miller's Store
N. Harvest
Church
Beechdale
START
Old Philadelphia Pike
340
Maple
N. Ronks
S. Harvest
Harvest
Irishtown
Old Leacock

**HOW** to get there  Take the Pennsylvania Turnpike to Lancaster/ Reading exit (exit 21). Go south on U.S. Route 222. Go east on U.S. Route 30 and then east on Route 340 for about 5 miles until you reach the Bird-In-Hand Farmers Market, where the ride starts. Or take U.S. Route 30 east of Lancaster to Route 896. Go north on Route 896 to Route 340. Then go east on Route 340 for about 3 miles to the farmer's market.

- Go to west end of farmers market parking lot, and go left on Maple Avenue.
- Right onto North Ronks Road at 0.4 mile.
- Left onto Irishtown Road at 0.7 mile.
- Left onto Old Leacock Road at 2.9 miles.
- Left onto Harvest /South Harvest Road at 3.7 miles.
- Right onto Old Philadelphia Pike (Route 340) at 5.5 miles.
- Left onto North Harvest Road at 5.6 miles.
- Straight through stop sign at 6.9 miles onto Newport Road.
- Left onto Scenic Road at 7.3 miles.
- Right and left, staying on Scenic, at 8.0 miles.
- Left onto Centerville Road at 8.7 miles.
- Left onto Zeltenreich Road at 10 miles.
- Right onto Musser School Road at 10.5 miles.
- Left onto Groffdale Road at 11.5 miles.
- Right onto East Eby Road at 11.7 miles.
- Left onto Stumptown Road at 12.7 miles.
- Left onto Monterey Road at 14.7 miles.
- Left to Miller's Store at 15.6 miles.
- Return to Monterey Road.
- Right onto Church Road at 15.9 miles.
- Left onto Beechdale Road at 16.8 miles.
- Left onto Old Philadelphia Pike (Route 340) at 17.1 miles.
- Right to finish at 17.2 miles.

such as quilts, chairs, and lamps. Because there's no middleman, the prices are generally rather low.

The first 5 miles of the ride take you through a succession of dairy farms. When you turn onto Harvest Road, you come to a large orchard. You'll see apples on your left and peaches on your right. If they look tempting, you can stop at Kauffman's Market, at the intersection of Old Philadelphia Pike and Harvest Road, to try them. Kauffman's has all sorts of stuff to refresh you, and there's even a picnic table under a tree.

On North Harvest Road is an Amish farm with a sign that says simply QUILTS. The lady of the house uses a manual sewing machine to produce quilts that she sells to customers all over the country.

On Newport Road you will find a one-room school. The Amish educate their children in these schools, and they're still building new ones.

Soon after you turn onto Scenic Road, you'll understand how it got its name. Although you will not have done any serious climbing, you'll have a great view of a little valley dotted with farms and silos. At the intersection of Stumptown and Mascot roads, there's a park on one side of the road. On the other side is the Mascot Roller Mill. Tours are available from May through October.

Natural-food fans will enjoy a visit to Miller's Store on Monterey Road. There's a green sign out front, just before a little stream. This is a well-stocked health-food store operated on an Amish farm. People drive a long way to stock up and save. Prices are considerably lower than in the mall. If you come during harvest months—July through October—you'll find big crates of pears, plums, apples, and other fruit sitting out front.

# Blue Ball

| | |
|---|---|
| **Number of miles:** | 13 or 19.6 |
| **Approximate pedaling time:** | 1 or 1½ hours |
| **Terrain:** | Rolling |
| **Surface:** | Fair, several rough spots |
| **Things to see:** | Farms, town of Churchtown, covered bridge, magnificent old houses |
| **Food:** | Shady Maple Market (at start and end) |
| **Facilities:** | Shady Maple Market |
| **Options:** | 6.6-mile extension; connection with New Holland ride |

On the roads around Blue Ball, the automobile is not king. In fact, it's probably number three in popularity, behind the horse and buggy and the bicycle. As you ride on these roads, you're likely to find more bikes than you'll see anywhere outside of China. The area has a large Mennonite population. Although Mennonites do have cars, they regard them primarily as utilitarian transport vehicles; so they often choose a bike over a car for a reasonably short trip.

This ride doesn't have any attractions that draw thousands of visitors along the way. What it offers is an opportunity to ride with minimal interference from cars. There's probably not a spot on this ride where you can't see at least one farm. If you ride on a summer morning, you'll find entire families working in the fields. The father may be on the tractor, while the mother and children pick crops, pull weeds, or put plants into the ground.

Early in the ride there is a covered bridge. If you've never ridden through one, be cautious. They're narrow and dark. Don't enter if there's a vehicle coming in the other direction.

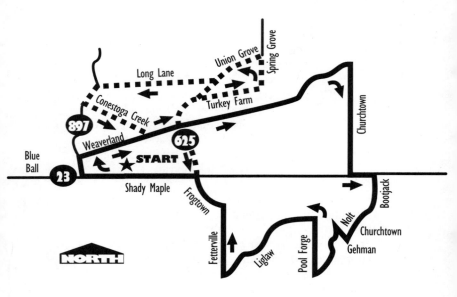

NOTE: ■ ■ ■ INDICATES RIDE EXTENSION

Spring Grove
Union Grove
Long Lane
Conestoga Creek
Turkey Farm
Churchtown
897
625
Weaverland
Blue Ball
23
★ START
Shady Maple
Frogtown
Bootjack
NORTH
Fetterville
Liglaw
Pool Forge
Nolt
Churchtown
Gehman

**HOW to get there** Shady Maple Market in Blue Ball, where you start, is on Route 23, between Routes 897 and 625, just east of Route 23's intersection with U.S. Route 322. Take the Pennsylvania Turnpike to the Morgantown exit. Get off the Turnpike and go west on Route 23.

**DIREC-TIONS for the ride**

- Leave the Shady Maple parking lot and go west (left) on Route 23.
- Right onto Route 897 at 0.5 mile.
- Right onto Weaverland Road at 0.9 mile.
- Bear left at fork, toward covered bridge, at 3.4 miles.
- Right onto Churchtown Road at 4.1 miles.
- Left onto Route 23 at 5.9 miles.
- Right onto Bootjack Road at 6.3 miles.
- Right onto Windsor Road at 6.5 miles.
- Left onto Churchtown Road at 7.0 miles.
- Right onto Nolt Road at 7.4 miles.
- Left onto Gehman Road at 7.6 miles.
- Right onto Pool Forge Road at 8.6 miles.
- Left onto Liglaw Road at 9.3 miles.
- Right onto Fetterville Road at 11.3 miles.
- Left onto Frogtown Road at 11.9 miles.
- Left onto Route 23 at 12.5 miles to Shady Maple.

## To extend the ride 6.6 miles

- After turning onto Route 23 (see direction above) turn right onto Route 625 at 12.7 miles.
- Right onto Turkey Farm Road at 13.8 miles.
- Left onto Spring Grove Road at 14.3 miles.
- Left onto Union Grove Road at 15.1 miles.
- Left onto Route 625 at 15.4 miles.
- Right onto Long Lane at 15.7 miles.
- Left onto Route 897 at 16.5 miles.
- Left onto Conestoga Creek Road at 16.9 miles.
- Left onto Weaverland Road at 18.0 miles.
- Right onto Route 625 at 18.3 miles.
- Right onto Route 23 at 19.1 miles.
- Finish at Shady Maple at 19.6 miles.

**Note:** You can easily connect this ride with the New Holland ride (ride 20). The place where they join is the intersection of Union Grove Road and Route 625. To pick up the New Holland ride, go straight instead of turning left onto Route 625. This will put you on Fairview Avenue, at the 8.4-mile mark of the New Holland ride.

---

Churchtown, the main settlement on the ride, is a small village named for its large number of churches. Today it sports antiques and craft shops. It also offers a great view of the valley to the north. On Windsor Road, just outside of Churchtown, stands one of the biggest houses that you'll see anywhere, but mostly you'll see farms.

This is a great place to ride for the sake of riding. And on a pristine autumn afternoon, this is as pretty a ride as can be.

The big day of the year in Blue Ball is Blue Ball Day, the Saturday before Labor Day. It's the town's big celebration. They have a pancake breakfast, a 5-mile run, crafts shows, and all sorts of entertainment and food. For at least that one day, the streets of Blue Ball are a busy place.

# Intercourse

| | |
|---:|:---|
| **Number of miles:** | 16.2 |
| **Approximate pedaling time:** | 1½ hours |
| **Terrain:** | Rolling |
| **Surface:** | Fair; be wary of ruts worn by horses |
| **Things to see:** | People's Place, Amish farms, covered bridge |
| **Food:** | Many places to eat in Intercourse; roadside produce stands |
| **Facilities:** | At Paradise Park |

This is a ride through lush Amish farmland, over lightly traveled roads. The little town of Intercourse is a curious melting pot. On Main Street you'll see Amish farmers buying supplies while visitors from all over the world buy souvenirs. You'll find horses and buggies tied up beside Cadillacs.

The primary tourist attraction in Intercourse is the People's Place, a group of shops featuring local Amish and Mennonite crafts. There's also a slide show that explains Amish life. Bikers passing through town often stop at Zimmerman's General Store for cold drinks.

You may encounter a little traffic on Route 340, but as soon as you turn onto West View Road, the serious traffic will end. Then it's farm after farm after farm. Keep your eyes open, though, and you'll notice signs advertising interesting items such as metal products, quilts, and even gravity boxes (old-fashioned manure spreaders). You'll also be likely to see farmers using teams of horses and mules to pull their plows and probably some horses and buggies. Keep in mind that a bicycle is generally faster than a buggy.

Spring Garden Road gives you a great downhill run. It's not espe-

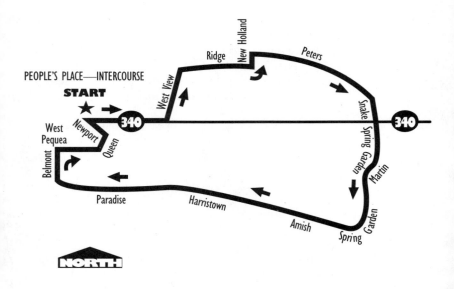

PEOPLE'S PLACE—INTERCOURSE

**START**

West View

Ridge

New Holland

Peters

Newport

West Pequea

Queen

Belmont

Snake

Spring Garden

Martin

340

340

Paradise

Harristown

Amish

Spring

Garden

**NORTH**

**HOW to get there**

Intercourse lies at the intersection of Routes 340 and 772, about 10 miles east of Lancaster. Route 340 runs north of and parallel to U.S. Route 30. Route 772 begins on Route 30, near Gap. The People's Place, where the ride begins, is right on Route 340.

- Leave the People's Place and go left on Route 340.
- Left onto West View Road at 1.0 mile.
- Right on Ridge Road at 2.0 miles.
- Left on New Holland Road at 3.4 miles.
- Right onto Peters Road at 3.5 miles.
- Right onto Snake Road at 5.9 miles.
- Merge into Spring Garden Road and cross Route 340 at 7.1 miles.
- Right onto Martin Road, and left onto Spring Garden Road at 7.6 miles.
- Right onto Amish Road at 8.7 miles.
- Right onto Harristown Road at 10.7 miles.
- Right onto Belmont Road at 13.2 miles.
- Right onto West Pequea (peck-way) Lane at 15.0 miles.
- Left onto Queen Road at 15.5 miles.
- Left onto Newport Road at 16.0 miles.
- Merge left into Old Philadelphia Pike (Route 340) to finish at 16.2 miles.

cially steep, but you should be able to hit 30 MPH without any effort. When you reach the intersection of Harristown and Belmont roads, you're in Paradise. To your left will be U.S. Route 30. After you turn onto Belmont, you'll see a covered bridge. Before you reach it, however, you'll see Londonvale Road on your left. If you're looking for a place to stop and relax, there's a nice park about half a mile down Londonvale Road.

Be careful going through the covered bridge. The boards go in the same direction as you're traveling, and it's possible to catch a tire and take a spill. If you're uncomfortable, it's best to walk the bike through. In case you're wondering, covered bridges got their covers to protect the wooden planks from the weather.

On Queen Lane is a woodworking shop that makes some very impressive weathervanes. At the end of the ride, be careful as you get back onto Route 340. It's a tricky intersection.

# **Lancaster County Covered Bridges**

| | |
|---:|:---|
| **Number of miles:** | 33.3 |
| **Approximate pedaling time:** | 3½ hours |
| **Terrain:** | Mostly rolling, several tough climbs |
| **Surface:** | Fair |
| **Things to see:** | Five covered bridges, America's oldest pretzel bakery, polo matches |
| **Food:** | Many places on route |
| **Facilities:** | In Lititz, Rothsville, Brownstown |

Lancaster County leads the nation in the covered-bridge category, with twenty-four bridges still in use. This ride takes you through five of them and on a tour of scenic farmlands.

The ride begins in Lititz, a tree-lined town that is home to the Sturgis Pretzel Bakery, the self-proclaimed first pretzel bakery in America. Established in 1861, the bakery allows visitors to watch pretzels being made and to twist their own. Lititz also features It's Only Natural, a natural foods store/macrobiotic restaurant on East Front Street, and the Wilbur Chocolate Company on North Broad Street, right beside Lititz Springs Park.

Just before you come to the first covered bridge, you'll see Hoover's Farm Market, an excellent source of farm-fresh produce. On Church Street in Rothsville is the Lancaster Polo Club. Matches take place on Sunday afternoons from May through September. Malcolm Forbes used to ride his motorcycle to Lancaster County to dine at the Brownstown Restaurant, at 10.6 miles.

At 14.7 miles you'll see a road sign that reads PASHING WEEG. Underneath is the English translation—PEACH ROAD. *Pashing weeg* is Pennsylvania Dutch, a German dialect spoken only in a small part of

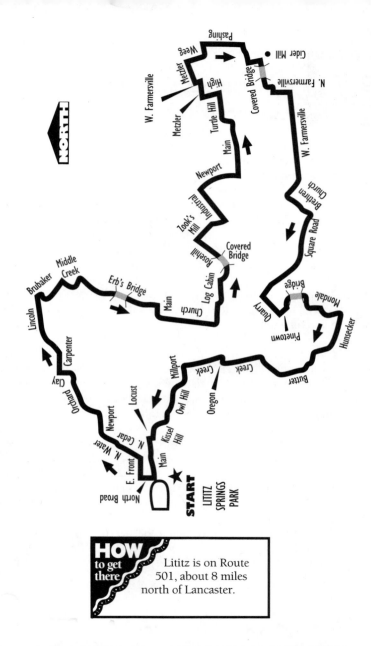

NORTH

Pashing
Weeg
Metzler
High
W. Farmersville
Metzler
Turtle Hill
Main
Newport
Zook's Mill
Industrial
Rosehill
Covered Bridge
Log Cabin
Church
Main
Erb's Bridge
Middle Creek
Brubaker
Lincoln
Carpenter
Clay
Orchard
Newport
N. Water
E. Front
North Broad
Main
N. Cedar
Locust
Kissel Hill
Owl Hill
Millport
Creek
Oregon
Creek
Creek
Butter
Hunsecker
Mondale
Bridge
Quarry
Pinetown
Square Road
Brethren
Church
W. Farmersville
N. Farmersville
Cider Mill
Covered Bridge

START

LITITZ SPRINGS PARK

HOW
to get
there

Lititz is on Route 501, about 8 miles north of Lancaster.

- Begin at Lititz Springs Park, on Route 501 in Lititz, beside the railroad tracks.
- Left (north) onto North Broad Street.
- Right onto East Front Street at 0.1 mile.
- Left onto North Cedar Street at 0.3 mile.
- Left onto North Water Street at 0.8 mile.
- Right onto Newport Road at 1.0 mile.
- Left onto Orchard Road at 1.3 miles.
- Left onto Clay Road at 2.5 miles.
- Right onto Carpenter Road at 2.8 miles.
- Straight onto Lincoln Road at 3.4 miles.
- Right onto Brubaker Road at 4.1 miles.
- Continue left on Brubaker Road at 4.2 miles.
- Right onto Middle Creek Road at 4.9 miles.
- Right onto Erb's Bridge Road at 5.1 miles.
- Covered Bridge at 5.5 miles.
- Right onto Main Street (Rothsville) at 6.8 miles.
- Left onto Church Street at 6.8 miles.
- Left onto Log Cabin Road at 8.0 miles.
- Covered Bridge at 9.0 miles.
- Left onto Rosehill Road after bridge at 9.0 miles.
- Right onto Zook's Mill Road at 9.4 miles.
- Left onto Industrial Road at 9.9 miles.
- Right onto Newport Road at 10.2 miles.
- Left onto Main Street (Brownstown) at 10.6 miles.
- Right onto Turtle Hill Road at 11.9 miles.
- Left onto High Road at 12.6 miles.
- Right onto Metzler Road at 13.1 miles.
- Left onto West Farmersville Road at 13.5 miles.
- Right onto Metzler Road at 13.6 miles.
- Right onto Pashing Weeg at 14.7 miles.
- Right onto Cider Mill Road at 15.3 miles.
- Covered Bridge at 15.7 miles.
- Right onto Covered Bridge at 15.8 miles.
- Left onto North Farmersville Road at 17.0 miles.

- Right onto West Farmersville Road at 17.4 miles.
- Left onto Brethren Church Road at 18.3 miles.
- Right onto Center Square Road at 19.1 miles.
- Right onto Quarry Road at 22.0 miles.
- Left onto Pinetown Road at 23.2 miles.
- Left onto Bridge Road at 23.7 miles.
- Covered Bridge at 23.7 miles.
- Right onto Mondale Road at 24.3 miles.
- Right onto Hunsecker Road at 25.4 miles.
- Right onto Butter Road at 26.3 miles.
- Butter Road becomes Creek Road.
- Cross Route 272 at 27.6 miles.
- Right onto Oregon Road at 28 miles.
- Immediate left onto Creek Road at 28 miles.
- Left onto Millport Road at 29.6 miles.
- Right onto Owl Hill Road at 29.7 miles.
- Right onto Kissel Hill Road at 31.8 miles.
- Right onto Locust Street at 32.4 miles.
- Left onto Main Street at 32.7 miles.
- Right onto North Broad Street at 33.2 miles, and finish at 33.3 miles.

---

Pennsylvania. It combines elements of English and German, and many of its speakers are Amish and Mennonite.

The third covered bridge presents the best chance to see a scene from one hundred years ago—a horse and buggy going through a covered bridge. Many Amish and Mennonite families live right around this bridge, and they travel primarily by buggy. At 17.4 miles you'll come to the four-way intersection of North/South Farmersville Road and East/West Farmersville Road.

The final two covered bridges on the ride took a beating from Hurricane Agnes in 1972. The Pinetown Bridge floated several miles downstream, but it remained intact, and workers managed to replace it. The raging waters destroyed the original Hunsecker Bridge, and a new one went up in 1975.

# Middle Creek

|  |  |
|---|---|
| **Number of miles:** | 16.4 |
| **Approximate pedaling time:** | 1½ hours |
| **Terrain:** | Rolling, with many flat sections |
| **Surface:** | Good |
| **Things to see:** | Middle Creek Wildlife Management Area, fertile farms |
| **Food:** | In Richland, halfway through ride |
| **Facilities:** | At visitors center at start of ride and at park in Richland |

This ride is definitely for bird lovers. Middle Creek Wildlife Management Area is a 5,000-acre preserve dedicated to the propagation and protection of wildlife, particularly geese and ducks. The most common species is the Canada goose. Thousands stop here to feed, and some make this their permanent home. The birds are most plentiful during their migratory flights in spring and fall. The preserve also has walking trails, picnic areas, and a visitors center. You might want to combine this bike ride with a hike. Outside the preserve, the farmlands and small towns of Lebanon County provide a nice place to ride with little traffic.

As you ride down Hopeland Road at the very beginning of the ride, you'll pass a big lake. Here you can see hundreds or thousands of birds—and probably some bird-watchers with binoculars. In addition to the geese, you may see bluebirds, swallows, redwings, and many more species. Even eagles have made occasional appearances. In the wooded areas there are many deer, and there have been several sightings of wild turkeys. But if you're unfamiliar with wildlife, don't worry; nothing around here will do you any harm.

At the end of Hopeland Road, you'll come to the tiny town of

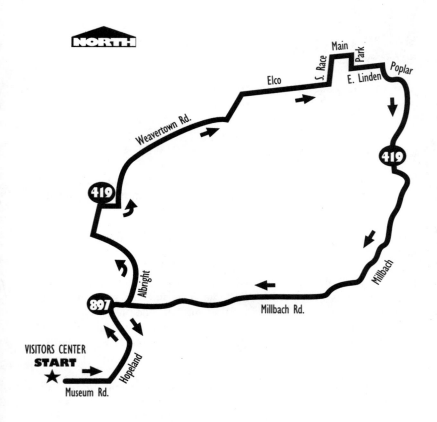

**NORTH**

Main

S. Race

Elco

Park

E. Linden

Poplar

Weavertown Rd.

419

419

Albright

Millbach

897

Millbach Rd.

VISITORS CENTER
**START**

Hopeland

Museum Rd.

**HOW to get there** Middle Creek Wildlife Management Area lies on Route 897, south of Lebanon. It can also be reached by U.S. Route 322. Take 322 west from Ephrata or east from Route 501 to Clay. Turn north on Clay Road and follow the signs to Middle Creek.

**DIREC-TIONS**
**for the ride**

- Leave the Middle Creek Visitors Center on Museum Road and go left on Hopeland Road, the main road through the preserve.
- Right onto Route 897 south at 2.5 miles.
- Left onto Albright Road at 2.6 miles.
- Bend to left at intersection with Chapel Road.
- Right on Route 419 (no sign) at T intersection at 4.8 miles.
- Left onto Weavertown Road (no sign) at 5.1 miles.
- Bear right on Weavertown at 5.9 miles.
- Right onto Elco Drive at 7.1 miles.
- Left onto South Race Avenue in Richland at 8.6 miles.
- Right onto Main Street (before tracks) at 8.9 miles.
- Right onto Park Street at 9.1 miles.
- Left onto East Linden Avenue at 9.4 miles.
- Right onto Poplar Street (toward Millbach) at 9.6 miles.
- Bend to left at 9.8 miles.
- Left onto Route 419 at T intersection at 11.3 miles.
- Right onto Millbach Road at 11.4 miles.
- Right onto Route 897 north at 14.0 miles.
- Left onto Hopeland Road at 14.1 miles.
- Right onto Museum Road at 16.4 miles.

Kleinfeltersville; then you'll move into farming territory. This is some of the most productive agricultural land in the world. If you come at the right time of year, you'll see fields bursting with corn, beans, melons, and much more. It wouldn't be a bad idea to bring a spoon, just in case you happen upon a good cantaloupe at one of the roadside stands.

About halfway through the ride, you'll come into Richland, a little town with a Norman Rockwell look to it. Here, you can get a brief glimpse of small-town life. You can park your bike and walk from one end of the business district to the other in a couple of minutes. You'll find food and cold drinks here.

After you pass through Richland, it's back into the country and more pleasant riding. You may even see a horse and buggy on the road.

# ICE HOUSE

THIS MASSIVE EXCAVATION WAS FILLED
WITH ICE BLOCKS CUT FROM THE ESTATE POND.
INSULATED WITH SAWDUST, IT
SUPPLIED ICE TO THE MANSION FOR ONE
FULL YEAR. SUSPENDED INSIDE ARE THE
ORIGINAL POLES USED TO RETRIEVE THE ICE.

# Mount Gretna/Mount Hope

| | |
|---:|:---|
| **Number of miles:** | 14.6 |
| **Approximate pedaling time:** | 1½ hours |
| **Terrain:** | Flat to rolling, with one steep hill |
| **Surface:** | Good |
| **Things to see:** | Mount Hope Winery, Renaissance Faire, Mount Gretna Playhouse, lake in Mount Gretna, Governor Dick Tower, Hampshire Orchards, Frey's Herb Farm |
| **Food:** | Store, bakery, and ice cream shop in Mount Gretna; apples and other fruit at Hampshire Orchards |
| **Facilities:** | At Mount Hope and in Mount Gretna |
| **Option:** | Connection with Speedwell Forge ride |

Here's a short ride with a lot of interesting sights along the way. Mount Hope, the former mansion of a wealthy, Early American iron-mine owner, is now a winery, and the grounds are a vineyard. Many different events take place on the grounds. On weekends from July through September, the Pennsylvania Renaissance Faire re-creates the splendor of sixteenth-century England. Hundreds of colorfully attired performers joust, juggle, and jest. There are also a Fifties Revival and a Dickens Christmas, in addition to wine making.

On Camp Road you'll see Hampshire Orchards. This is an unusual orchard in that it's basically new. Its thousands of neatly planted young trees were just coming into full production in 1989. Here you can get apples and peaches directly from the trees, as well as freshly made cider and other apple products. Just down the road is Frey's Herb Farm, a good place to stock up on parsley, sage, thyme, and so on.

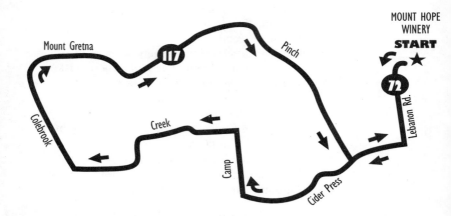

MOUNT HOPE
WINERY
**START**

Mount Gretna

117

Pinch

Colebrook

Creek

Camp

Cider Press

Lebanon Rd.

72

**HOW**
to get
there

Take the Pennsylvania Turnpike to the
Lancaster/Lebanon exit. Exit onto Route 72
and go south, toward Lancaster. Mount Hope
Estate is right beside the turnpike, on Route 72,
north of Lancaster and south of Lebanon.

**DIREC-TIONS for the ride**

- Leave the parking lot at Mount Hope and go left (south) on Route 72 (Lebanon Road).
- Right on Cider Press Road at 0.5 mile.
- Right onto Camp Road at 3.2 miles.
- Left onto Creek Road at 3.7 miles.
- Right onto Colebrook Road at 5.4 miles.
- Right onto Mount Gretna Road (Route 117) at 7.9 miles.
- Right onto Pinch Road at 10.8 miles.
- Left onto Cider Press Road at 13.6 miles.
- Left onto Route 72 (Lebanon Road) at 14.1 miles.
- Right into Mount Hope at 14.6 miles.

**Note:** You can easily connect this ride with the Speedwell Forge ride (ride 22). To do so, when you hit Route 72 (Lebanon Road) at the 14.1-mile mark, go straight onto Mountain Road instead of turning left. Three miles down Mountain Road, you'll come to Sanctuary Road, which is the 5.2-mile mark of the Speedwell Forge ride.

For a while the ride rolls through farms and a golf course. On Colebrook Road you'll climb a little, cross over the Pennsylvania Turnpike, and move into a section of state game land. The farms will end, and the woods will begin.

Mount Gretna is an appealing little town with something to interest almost everyone. The lake, open for public swimming, is inviting on a hot day. It must also be inviting on New Year's Day, because several hundred "Polar Bears" dive in every year, even when they have to break the ice to do so. During the summer, Mount Gretna is a vacation home for some families. Its main attractions are its quiet and events such as art shows. There's also a playhouse with a full summer schedule and an equally busy concert series. For refreshments, there are an ice cream shop and a general store. There's also an antiques shop. If you were to wake up and find yourself in Mount Gretna, you'd probably think that you were somewhere in New England.

Although you can't see many of them from the main road, there are some magnificent houses in Gretna, tucked away among the evergreen trees that cover most of the area. To see them, go up any of the side streets to your right.

You'll hit the ride's one good hill as you leave Gretna on Pinch Road. But it's not all bad. At the top of the hill is a big stone slab with a marker commemorating Governor Dick, and if you follow the trail, you come to a big tower that you can climb for a great view of the surrounding valleys.

# New Holland

| | |
|---|---|
| **Number of miles:** | 47 or 15.1 |
| **Approximate pedaling time:** | 4½ hours or 1½ hours |
| **Terrain:** | Some of everything—flat stretches to good hills |
| **Surface:** | Fair |
| **Things to see:** | Pennsylvania Dutch country, Amish farms, antiques shops, small towns, zoo |
| **Food:** | In New Holland, Terre Hill, Bowmansville, Adamstown, and Martindale |
| **Facilities:** | At parks in New Holland, Terre Hill, Adamstown, and Bowmansville |
| **Options:** | Detour back to start for shorter ride, connection with Blue Ball ride |

This is a longer ride that will take you through the farmland of eastern Lancaster County. (For less ambitious riders, there's an optional shorter ride of 15.1 miles.) Many of these farms are owned and operated by the "Plain People," Amish and Mennonites. Members of these religious sects avoid modern conveniences such as cars or electricity.

The terrain makes this a fairly difficult ride. Around Adamstown and Bowmansville, it's quite hilly. But there are no hills that a strong rider can't handle.

New Holland is the first and the last town on the ride. This is a busy place where Plain People mix with their "English" neighbors. The biggest industry in town is the Ford New Holland plant, where they produce the most modern of farm equipment. Ironically, the plant sits right beside Amish farms that still use horses to pull the plows. At the New Holland Community Park, where the ride begins,

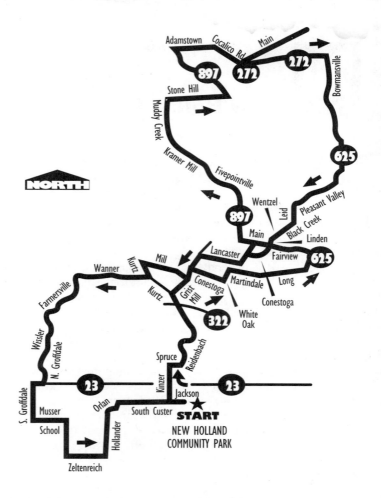

**HOW to get there**

New Holland is on Route 23, about 10 miles northeast of Lancaster. Route 23 intersects U.S. Route 30 in Lancaster and U.S. Route 322 in Blue Ball. Take the Pennsylvania Turnpike at Morgantown exit and go west on Route 23. At the Kinzer Avenue traffic light in New Holland, go south (left) on Kinzer Avenue. The New Holland Community Park, where the ride starts, is one block south of Route 23, on Jackson Street.

**DIREC-TIONS for the ride**

- From New Holland Community Park parking area, go left on Jackson Street.
- Right onto Kinzer Avenue at 0.1 mile.
- Right onto Spruce Avenue at 0.8 mile.
- Left onto Reidenbach Road at 0.9 mile.
- Reidenbach Road bends right at 1.5 miles.
- Cross U.S. Route 322 onto Kurtz Road, at 3.0 miles.

**Note:** At this point you can opt to take a shorter ride (15.1 miles) by first following these two directions:

- Left onto Wanner Road at 3.8 miles.
- Cross U.S. Route 322 at 4.7 miles.

Then skip the next thirty-five directions. Pick the directions up again at "Merge straight onto Farmersville Road." (For the rest of the directions, mileage for the shorter option is given in parentheses.)

- Right onto Grist Mill Road at 3.4 miles.
- Right onto Conestoga Road at 4.4 miles.
- Left onto White Oak Road at 5.2 miles.
- Right onto Martindale Road at 5.5 miles.
- Left onto Long Lane at 6.0 miles.
- Left onto Route 625 at 8.0 miles.
- Left onto Fairview Avenue (at Terre Hill Mennonite School) at 8.4 miles.
- Fairview becomes Main Street.
- Left onto Conestoga Avenue at 9.8 miles.
- Go through park and right onto Lancaster Avenue.
- Left onto Main Street.
- Right onto Route 897.
- Left onto Fivepointville Road at 12.2 miles.
- Right onto Kramer Mill Road at 12.9 miles.
- Right onto Muddy Creek Road at 14.7 miles.
- Right onto Stone Hill Road at 15.9 miles.
- Left at T intersection (Route 897) at 17.2 miles.

- Right onto Adamstown Road at 20.0 miles.
- Right onto Cocalico Road at 20.7 miles (white buildings to your right).
- Straight on Route 272 at 21.0 miles.
- Bear left at swimming pool at 21.3 miles.
- Right onto Bowmansville Road at 22.6 miles.
- Right onto Route 625 south at 26.3 miles. (For park in Bowmansville, turn left on Church Road.)
- Right onto Pleasant Valley Road at 27.7 miles.
- Left onto Leid Road at 29.0 miles.
- Right onto Black Creek Road at 29.8 miles.
- Right onto Wentzel Road at 30.8 miles.
- Left onto Linden Avenue at 31.3 miles.
- Right onto Main Street at 31.6 miles.
- Left onto Conestoga Avenue (through park again) at 32.0 miles.
- Left onto Lancaster Avenue.
- Left onto Grist Mill Road at 34.3 miles.
- Right onto Mill Road at 34.5 miles.
- Left onto Kurtz Road at 35.3 miles.
- Right onto Wanner Road at 35.6 miles.
- Merge straight onto Farmersville Road at 36.8 miles.
- Farmersville Road bends right at 37.2 miles.
- Left onto Wissler Road at 37.6 miles.
- Merge straight onto North Groffdale Road at 39.6 (7.8) miles.
- Right onto Route 23 at 40.9 (9.1) miles.
- Left onto South Groffdale Road at 41.0 (9.2) miles.
- Left onto Musser School Road at 41.8 (10.0) miles.
- Left onto Zeltenreich Road at 42.9 (11.1) miles.
- Left onto Hollander Road at 43.9 (12.1) miles.
- Right onto Orlan Road at 45.0 (13.2) miles.
- Left onto South Custer Avenue at 45.7 (14.0) miles.
- Right onto West Jackson at 46.0 (14.2) miles.
- Finish at 47.0 (15.1) miles.

**Note:** You can connect this ride with the Blue Ball ride (ride 15). They join at the intersection of Route 625 and Union Grove Road. To pick up the Blue Ball ride, go right on Union Grove Road instead of going left on Fairview Avenue at 8.4 miles. This will put you at the 15.1 mile mark of the Blue Ball ride.

---

there's a full summer schedule of events such as concerts. In early October the New Holland Fair takes over the town. Ferris wheels, food, and agricultural exhibits fill the streets.

You'll leave New Holland and pass through flat farm country for a few miles. The next community is Terre Hill. This is a quiet little place with several restaurants, some beautiful old homes, and a nice little park.

After passing through Terre Hill, you'll be out in farming country for about 10 miles. The next major settlement will be Adamstown. In August Adamstown is home to the Gemütlichkeit (*guh-moot-lick-kite*), sometimes called the Bavarian Beer Festival. On Sundays throughout the year, Adamstown is a major antiques center. Vendors seem to set up almost anywhere.

Down the road from Adamstown is Bowmansville, known to locals as the home of the Ox Trot, a particularly hilly 5-mile running race held on the second Saturday in August. In Bowmansville there are a general store, a park, and a youth hostel.

From Bowmansville you'll go back through Terre Hill and then back to New Holland, but mostly on different roads. All along the way you can expect to see a lot of bicycles. Among the people in this area, the bike is a primary means of transportation. And they don't ride sleek twelve-speeds; three-speeds are much more common. On a Sunday morning you'll see hundreds of young people riding bikes to and from church. Any day of the week, if you hit a traffic jam, it will be more likely to involve buggies and bikes than cars. Many of the cars that you do see will be black. Some will even have black bumpers. Mennonites paint their cars this way as a religious statement.

As you ride, you'll pass many farms. Most will have stands offering produce and baked goods. Many will also sell such local specialties as shoo-fly pie and homemade root beer.

# Quarryville

| | |
|---:|:---|
| **Number of miles:** | 21 |
| **Approximate pedaling time:** | 2 hours |
| **Terrain:** | Rolling, several good hills |
| **Surface:** | Good |
| **Things to see:** | Amish farms, scenic vistas, covered bridge |
| **Food:** | In Quarryville and Bartville |
| **Facilities:** | At start of ride and in Bartville |

Quarryville is the only significant town in southern Lancaster County, and the surrounding area offers some great bicycling. Amish families live on many of the farms, and because they travel in buggies, traffic is generally quite light. Quarryville took its name from the many quarries in the area. The limestone that makes the soil rich also makes good stone for building.

Tourists have discovered the other Amish areas of Lancaster County, but the southern end is far off the paths of most visitors. From June until October the predominant feature of the landscape is corn. It covers thousands of acres, and at times it's all that you can see as you ride along. In good years it towers above even the tallest people.

The covered bridge on this ride offers some interesting pictures in hot weather, when cows and horses gather under it to get out of the sun. The Bartville Store, at 7.2 miles, is your only source of supplies on the ride. It's a fairly unusual store in that it has both gas pumps and places for the Amish to tie their horses.

Robert Fulton Highway takes its name from the inventor of the steamboat. His birthplace is about 5 miles south of Quarryville along the highway.

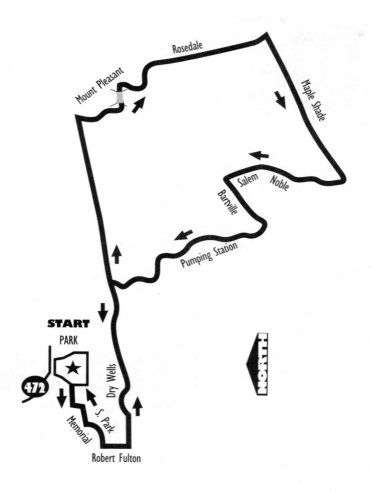

Rosedale

Mount Pleasant

Maple Shade

Salem    Noble

Barrville

Pumping Station

START

PARK

★

472

Dry Wells

S. Park

Memorial

Robert Fulton

NORTH

**HOW**
**to get**
**there**

Quarryville is about 12 miles south of Lancaster, in southern Lancaster County, at the intersection of U.S. Route 222, Route 372, and Route 472.

**DIREC-TIONS for the ride**

- Start at Quarryville Park, Route 472, on the south side of town. Begin at the Hoffman Community Building. Go west toward the swimming pool.
- Left onto Memorial Drive at 0.1 mile.
- Left onto South Park Avenue at 0.2 mile.
- Left onto Robert Fulton Highway at 0.8 mile (caution, busy road).
- Left onto Dry Wells Road at 0.9 mile.
- Right onto Mount Pleasant Road at 5.4 miles.
- Left after covered bridge at 6.1 miles.
- Bear right, uphill, at 6.6 miles.
- Straight ahead on Rosedale Road at 7.2 miles (Bartville Store).
- Right onto Maple Shade Road at 9.2 miles.
- Right onto Noble Road at 11.9 miles.
- Left onto Salem Road at 13.6 miles.
- Left onto Bartville Road at 14.2 miles.
- Right onto Pumping Station Road at 15.1 miles.
- Left onto Dry Wells Road at 17.4 miles.
- Right onto Robert Fulton Highway at 20.1 miles.
- Right onto South Park Avenue at 20.2 miles.
- Right onto Memorial Drive at 20.8 miles.
- Finish at 21.0 miles.

# Speedwell Forge

| | |
|---:|:---|
| **Number of miles:** | 25 |
| **Approximate pedaling time:** | 1¾ hours |
| **Terrain:** | Rolling hills |
| **Surface:** | Good |
| **Things to see:** | Farms and woods |
| **Food:** | Produce stand on Fairview Road, at 17.5 miles |
| **Facilities:** | At Speedwell Forge Lake and one-room school on Lexington Road |
| **Option:** | Connection with Mount Gretna/Mount Hope ride |

This ride is the course that's used for the Lancaster YMCA Triathlon. It's very scenic, surely one of the prettiest rides in all the triathlon world, and slightly hilly. And because it's laid out to be a racecourse, you can cover it without having to make a lot of stops. It's 25 fast miles. If you're interested in seeing how fast you can do it, and in comparing yourself to the triathletes, keep in mind that the best riders do this course in about an hour. But they do have the advantage of having traffic stopped at all the intersections.

As you begin the ride, you pass the upper end of Speedwell Forge Lake. You may see some ducks and geese along here. A little farther down the road, just past Long Lane, is a farm where they raise horses and even have a small arena for showing horses. One of the residents of this farm is a peacock. He likes to strut his stuff by the side of the road.

At 2.3 miles you'll turn onto Mountain Road. Don't let the name alarm you; the road has a hill but nothing resembling a mountain. And it also has a great view of the Pennsylvania Turnpike. You can

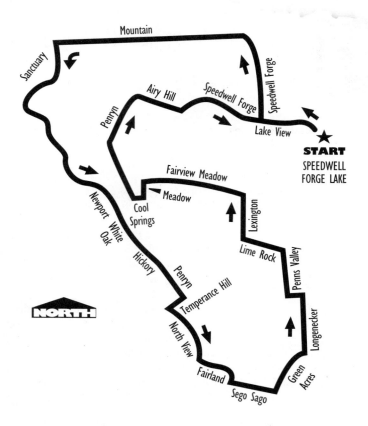

Mountain

Sanctuary

Airy Hill

Speedwell Forge

Speedwell Forge

Penryn

Lake View

★
**START**

SPEEDWELL
FORGE LAKE

Fairview Meadow

Meadow

Cool
Springs

Lexington

Newport White Oak

Lime Rock

Penns Valley

Hickory

Penryn

Temperance Hill

Longenecker

North View

Fairland

Green Acres

Sego Sago

**NORTH**

**HOW to get there**   Speedwell Forge Lake is just west of Route 501, north of Lititz and south of Route 501's intersection with U.S. Route 322. There are signs to it; the ride begins at the lake parking area. You can also reach the lake by getting off the Pennsylvania Turnpike at the Lancaster/Lebanon interchange and going south to Route 72. Then go right on Mountain Road, right on Speedwell Forge Road, and left on Lake View Road to the parking area.

**DIREC-TIONS**
**for the ride**

**Note:** While you're riding along this route, you'll see arrows and mile markers painted on the road. If you wish to follow them, look for mile markers that say LONG BIKE.

- From the parking area at Speedwell Forge Lake, go north, the only possible way, on Lake View Road.
- Merge right onto Speedwell Forge Road at 1.0 mile.
- Left onto Mountain Road at 2.3 miles.
- Left onto Sanctuary Road at 5.2 miles.
- Bear right, staying on Sanctuary, at 5.9 miles.
- Bear left, staying on Sanctuary, at 6.2 miles.
- Left onto Newport Road at 6.5 miles.
- Straight onto White Oak Road at 6.8 miles.
- Left onto Hickory Road at 8.3 miles.
- Right onto Penryn Road at 8.9 miles.
- Right onto Temperance Hill Road at 10.9 miles.
- Left onto North View Road at 11.1 miles.
- Left on Fairland Road at 12.0 miles.
- Left onto Sego Sago Road at 12.7 miles.
- Left onto Green Acres Road at 13.4 miles.
- Left onto Longenecker Road at 13.9 miles.
- Left onto Temperance Hill Road at 14.7 miles.
- Right onto Penns Valley Road at 14.8 miles.
- Left onto Lime Rock Road at 15.0 miles.
- Bear right, across railroad tracks, onto Lexington Road at 15.5 miles.
- Left and right, staying on Lexington, at 16.8 miles.
- Left onto Fairview Road at 17.5 miles.
- Left onto Meadow Road at 19.5 miles.
- Right onto Cool Springs Road at 20.0 miles.
- Right onto Penryn Road at 20.3 miles.
- Right onto Airy Hill Road at 22.8 miles.
- Left onto Speedwell Forge Road at 23.5 miles.

- Sharp right onto Lake View Road at 24.6 miles.
- Finish at 25.6 miles.

**Note:** This ride connects easily to the Mount Gretna/Mount Hope Ride (ride 19). To make the connection, at the 5.2 mile mark, instead of turning left on Sanctuary Road, go straight on Mountain Road. This will take you to Route 72. When you reach Route 72, you can turn right and go half a mile to the Mount Hope Estate and the beginning of the Mount Gretna/Mount Hope ride, or you can cross Route 72 onto Cider Press Road and pick up the ride there.

---

look with compassion on the people trapped in their gasoline monsters.

There aren't any tourist attractions on this ride. You'll just ramble along on country roads amid corn fields, soybean fields (they're the hairy little pods), cows, and sheep. It's not unusual to ride for three to five minutes without seeing a car.

On Lexington Road you'll see a little green, one-room schoolhouse. There are outhouses behind the school if you really need them. On Fairview Road is a fruit stand where the fruits and vegetables from the adjacent farm are sold.

After that it's more country roads to the finish. Be careful on Speedwell Forge Road at the end of the ride. You go down a steep hill and have to make a very sharp right. Don't try to take the turn at high speed.

# Strasburg

| | |
|---:|:---|
| **Number of miles:** | 14.5 |
| **Approximate pedaling time:** | 1½ hours |
| **Terrain:** | Rolling |
| **Surface:** | Fair |
| **Things to see:** | Strasburg RailRoad, Railroad Museum of Pennsylvania, Toy Train Museum, Amish farms, verdant valley |
| **Food:** | At beginning of ride and in Strasburg |
| **Facilities:** | At beginning and end of ride; none on course |

This is a ride on which it seems that there's always something interesting to see. There are tourist attractions and beautiful scenery. And there are country roads with very little traffic.

The Strasburg RailRoad, the starting point for the ride, is the first point of interest. This is America's oldest short-line railroad. The train ride it offers won't really take you anywhere, but it's a nice way to see the farm country between Strasburg and Paradise. The trains are open-air cars pulled by old coal-burning engines. Adjacent to the Strasburg RailRoad is the Railroad Museum of Pennsylvania, with a large collection of trains and related items. If you're a real train lover, you can spend a night at the Red Caboose Motel; all the rooms are actual cabooses.

As you head out on the ride, you'll be able to keep pace with the trains, and you'll cross the tracks several times. If you carry your camera, you can get some nice pictures. The rail line goes through one of the prettiest farm areas anywhere. The small farms form a patchwork quilt of brown earth and green crops. As you ride east

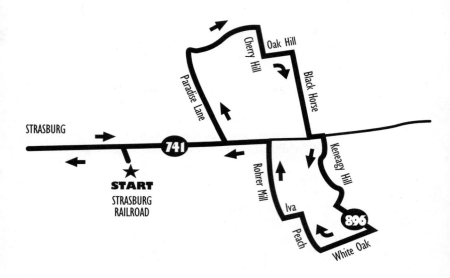

Oak Hill

Cherry Hill

Paradise Lane

Black Horse

STRASBURG

**741**

★ **START**
STRASBURG
RAILROAD

Rohrer Mill

Keneagy Hill

Iva

**896**

Peach

White Oak

**HOW** to get there   Strasburg is at the intersection of Routes 741 and 896, about 10 miles southeast of Lancaster. Route 896 intersects U.S. Route 30; Route 741 intersects U.S. Route 222 and Route 41. To reach the start of the ride at the Strasburg RailRoad, take Route 741 east from Strasburg center.

- From the Strasburg RailRoad, head east on Route 741.
- Left on Paradise Lane at 0.5 mile.
- Paradise Lane turns right at 1.8 miles.
- Right onto Cherry Hill Lane at 3.1 miles.
- Left onto Oak Hill Road at 3.8 miles.
- Right onto Black Horse Road at 4.2 miles.
- Left onto Route 741 at 5.7 miles.
- Right onto Keneagy Hill Road at 5.7 miles.
- Left onto Route 896 at T intersection at 7.4 miles.
- Right onto White Oak Road at 8.1 miles.
- Right onto Peach Road at 8.5 miles.
- Left onto Iva Road (sharp turn at bottom of hill) at 9.5 miles.
- Right onto Rohrer Mill Road at 9.9 miles.
- Cross Route 896 at 10.3 miles.
- Left onto Route 741 (Strasburg Road) at 11.3 miles.
- Straight to traffic light in Strasburg 13.5 miles.
- Turn around and return to Strasburg RailRoad 14.5 miles.

from Strasburg, you'll notice that green is the dominant color. The valley is incredibly lush and verdant.

Many of the farms belong to Amish families and are meticulously neat and exceptionally productive. On the roads you're bound to come up behind a horse and buggy somewhere, and you'll find produce being sold directly from the farms. There is no sweeter sweet corn anywhere.

The ride includes one good hill, on Keneagy Hill Road. But the view from the top makes the little climb worthwhile.

The end of the ride brings you into the small, historic town of Strasburg. Many of the buildings sport plaques that indicate their historic importance. In town you'll find many places to eat and a variety of shops. There are a general store, a baseball card shop, and antiques shops. Strasburg is a good place to find Amish arts and crafts and relax after your ride.

# Biglerville

| | |
|---:|:---|
| **Number of miles:** | 17 |
| **Approximate pedaling time:** | 1¾ hours |
| **Terrain:** | Mostly flat, some rolling hills |
| **Surface:** | Good |
| **Things to see:** | Apple orchards, Penn State Fruit Research Farm, Apple Blossom Festival, Apple Harvest Festival |
| **Food:** | Jane's Market and restaurants in Biglerville; General Store in Arendtsville |
| **Facilities:** | At Oak Park (15.5 miles) |

The best time to take this ride is from late April into early May when the fruit trees blossom. At several points on the ride, apple, peach, pear, and cherry trees will be all that you can see. Adams County is the heart of Pennsylvania's fruit-growing region, and Biglerville is the center for the production of apple products. Several big companies, such as Musselman's, have plants here. Pedaling through this quiet, scenic area can be a delight.

The ride begins in downtown Biglerville, a metropolis of perhaps 2,000. In less than a mile, you're out of town and on a country road that winds through farms and crosses a gentle stream. For several miles you'll see typical farmland. Then, after you go through the town of Arendtsville, you'll enter serious orchard territory. These orchards are a breathtaking sight when all the trees are in bloom. As you ride, you'll see a mountain looming to the west, but you'll never have to climb it: The ride stays in the valley.

In addition to the cultivated fruits, you'll also find wild raspberries all along the ride. The black ones ripen first, in late June and

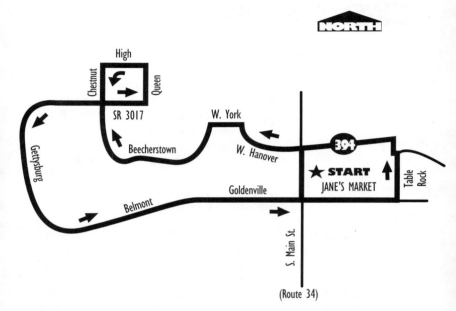

NORTH

High
Chestnut
Queen
SR 3017
W. York
Gettysburg
Beecherstown
W. Hanover
394
★ START
JANE'S MARKET
Table Rock
Goldenville
Belmont
S. Main St.
(Route 34)

**HOW to get there**
Biglerville is 8 miles north of Gettysburg and 30 miles south of Carlisle on Route 34. Gettysburg is on U.S. Route 30. Carlisle is on Interstate 81. To reach the start of the ride at Jane's Market in Biglerville, follow Route 34 about two blocks south of the main intersection in town.

**DIREC-TIONS**
**for the ride**

- Leave the Jane's Market parking lot and go north (right) on South Main Street (Route 34).
- Left onto West Hanover Street (Route 394 west) at 0.2 mile.
- Left onto West York Street (Route 234 west) at 0.7 mile.
- Left onto Beecherstown Road at 0.9 mile.
- Right onto Gettysburg Street (SR 3017) at 4.1 miles.
- Left onto Queen Street at 4.7 miles.
- Left onto High Street at 4.8 miles.
- Left onto Chestnut Street at 5.3 miles.
- Right onto Gettysburg Street at 5.4 miles.
- Left onto Belmont Road at 9.7 miles.
- Right onto Goldenville Road at 11.4 miles.
- Cross Route 34 at 12.3 miles.
- Left onto Table Rock Road at 12.9 miles.
- Straight onto Route 394 west at stop sign, at 14.6 miles.
- Left onto South Main at 16.7 miles.
- Return to Jane's at 17.0 miles.

early July. The red ones appear around the middle of July. Cherries begin to ripen in the middle of June; peaches, pears, and apples toward the end of July. Different varieties come into their prime all the way through October.

This is a ride without any major tourist attractions along the way. Just off the route, however, is the site of the Apple Blossom Festival (early April) and Apple Harvest Festival (first two weekends in October). These take place at South Mountain Fairgrounds on Route 34 west of Arendtsville. The fairgrounds are easy to reach. When the ride directions indicate a left turn on High Street in Arendtsville, go right instead. You'll see the fairgrounds about 2 miles down on Route 34 North.

As a whole this ride is scenic and and low on traffic. The closest ride is Gettysburg (ride 25), which is about 8 miles south on Route 34.

# Gettysburg

| | |
|---:|:---|
| **Number of miles:** | 17 |
| **Approximate pedaling time:** | 2 hours |
| **Terrain:** | Rolling, several good hills |
| **Surface:** | Good |
| **Things to see:** | Gettysburg Battlefield, Eisenhower Farm |
| **Food:** | Many restaurants near start and finish of ride; several on Howard Avenue, near 14-mile mark on tour |
| **Facilities:** | At visitors center and several places on battlefield |

From July 1 to July 3, 1863, the small Pennsylvania town of Gettysburg gained lasting fame. During those three days of the Civil War, the bloodiest battle in the history of North America raged over farm fields and through the town. On November 18, 1863, President Abraham Lincoln delivered his famous Gettysburg Address here. Today the Gettysburg National Military Park offers a great opportunity to bicycle through history.

Many parts of the battlefield are almost the same today as they were on the evening of July 3, 1863. Fences, cannons, and rocks have not been moved. But there have been many additions: monuments, observation towers, and educational displays.

The ride is a very pretty one. The fields are green and surrounded by woodland. In the spring, the pink blossoms of the dogwood trees, the yellow of the dandelions, and the purple of the violets turn the battlefield into a blaze of color. And while this was briefly a battlefield, today there's a powerful feeling of serenity in the air.

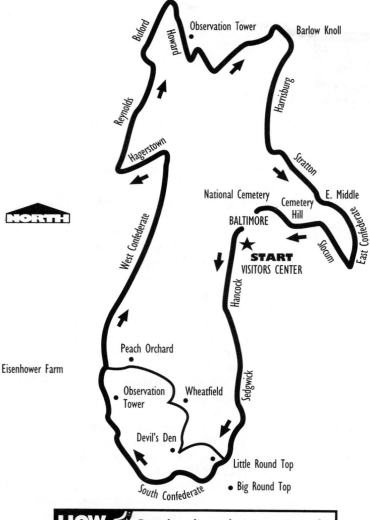

NORTH

Buford
Howard
Observation Tower
Barlow Knoll
Harrisburg
Reynolds
Stratton
Hagerstown
National Cemetery
E. Middle
Cemetery Hill
BALTIMORE
West Confederate
Slocum
East Confederate
★ START
VISITORS CENTER
Hancock
Eisenhower Farm
Peach Orchard
Observation Tower
Wheatfield
Sedgwick
Devil's Den
Little Round Top
South Confederate
Big Round Top

**HOW** to get there  Gettysburg lies at the intersections of U.S. Routes 30 and 15 and at the intersection of U.S. Route 30 and Route 34. The Gettysburg Visitors Center is just south of the town square on Baltimore Avenue.

**DIREC-TIONS for the ride**

The best method is to follow the signs. They'll guide you all around the battlefield.

- Leaving the visitors center, go right onto Hancock Avenue.
- Hancock becomes Sedgwick.
- Right onto South Confederate Avenue.
- South Confederate becomes West Confederate.
- Left onto Hagerstown Road.
- Left onto Reynolds Avenue.
- Reynolds becomes Buford Avenue.
- Right onto Howard Avenue.
- Right onto Harrisburg Road.
- Harrisburg Road becomes Stratton Street.
- Left onto East Middle Street.
- Right onto East Confederate Avenue.
- Right onto Slocum Avenue.
- Right onto Baltimore Street.
- Return to visitors center.

At the park visitors center you can see exhibits and mementos and pick up a brochure that will guide you on your tour. There are tours listed for cars and for bikes. The auto tour is better; it's 17 miles, and it covers the entire battlefield. The bike tour is only about 6 miles.

The first stop on the tour is the High Water Mark. It was here that Union soldiers stopped the advance of General George E. Pickett and his troops. This effectively ended the Battle of Gettysburg and sent the Confederates into retreat.

As you continue on Hancock Avenue, you'll come to the Pennsylvania Memorial. This monument pays tribute to the 35,000 Pennsylvanians who fought here. Hancock turns into Sedgwick Avenue, which turns into Confederate Avenue. There are signs all along the way. The best view is available at Little Round Top. From here, you can get a look at much of the battle area.

The Eisenhower Farm, home of former President Dwight Eisenhower, is just west of Confederate Avenue, but they won't let you bike through it. It's accessible only by shuttle buses that leave from the visitors center.

On West Confederate Avenue is an observation tower that you can climb for a great view of the area. There's also a tower close to the visitors center. It's bigger, but it costs money. The one on West Confederate is free.

Throughout this ride be wary of cars. They generally move slowly, but often the drivers are looking at the monuments instead of the road. Allow plenty of time for the ride. You'll probably want to stop and look frequently.

# Newport

| | |
|---:|:---|
| **Number of miles:** | 17 |
| **Approximate pedaling time:** | $1\frac{1}{2}$ hours |
| **Terrain:** | One good hill, otherwise flat to rolling |
| **Surface:** | Good |
| **Things to see:** | Little Buffalo State Park, trees, streams, birds, animals |
| **Food:** | General store (4.5 miles); restaurants and stores in Newport |
| **Facilities:** | At Little Buffalo State Park, general store, and various places in Newport |

If you love nightlife and crowds of people, you'll feel lost on this ride. There are probably more people living on some blocks in New York City than there are in all of Perry County. And although Perry County comes within a mile of Harrisburg, it has remained rural and unspoiled. In fact, the county still doesn't have a traffic light. Most of the region is still forest, with some farms mixed in.

Little Buffalo State Park offers all sorts of outdoor activities: camping, swimming, boating, and hiking. The ride begins there and heads west on Little Buffalo Creek Road. The road is relatively flat, although the hills rise steeply beside it. The only tough hill on the ride comes after you go right on SR 4005 at about 3.5 miles. You'll have a decent climb, then you'll drop down into a valley and meander along a creek.

The big town on the ride is Newport. This is the kind of place where neighbors know one another, and you can walk from one end of the shopping district to the other in about five minutes. The main road into town is U.S. Route 322/22. This is a road that owes its four-

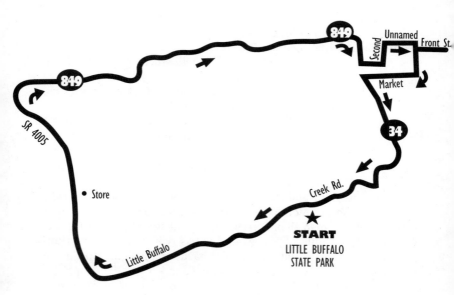

849
Second
Unnamed
Front St.
849
Market
SR 4005
34
Store
Creek Rd.
★
START
LITTLE BUFFALO
STATE PARK
Little Buffalo

**HOW to get there** Little Buffalo State Park, where the ride begins, is on Little Buffalo Creek Road, about 2 miles west of Route 34, just south of Newport. To get to Newport, take U.S. Route 322/22 out of Harrisburg. Then go south on Route 34 and look for signs for Little Buffalo State Park.

- Leave the park office at Little Buffalo State Park and go west on Little Buffalo Creek Road.
- Right (toward Skyline Corner General Store) onto SR 4005 at end of Little Buffalo Creek Road.
- Straight through intersection at 4.5 miles.
- Right onto Route 849 east at 5.9 miles.
- Left onto Market Street at 13.2 miles.
- Left onto Second Street at 13.3 miles.
- Right onto unnamed street at 13.6 miles (look for baseball fields).
- Right onto Front Street at 13.7 miles.
- Right onto Market Street at 13.9 miles.
- Left onto Second Street (Route 34 south) at 14.0 miles.
- Right onto Little Buffalo Creek Road at 15.0 miles (signs to park).
- Right to Park Office at 17.0 miles.

lane status to Penn State football. Although politicians may argue otherwise, the road was improved in order to carry fans from the eastern half of the state to State College. When the Nittany Lions aren't playing, there's not a lot of traffic out on the highway. It's also one of the prettiest roads anywhere, as its two-tier construction affords great views of the Juniata (not Juanita) River.

This is a great ride for getting away from it all. It's very pretty and very quiet. If you come in the autumn, it's really spectacular. If you're interested in a longer ride, stop at the office at Little Buffalo State Park. The staff has maps of the county, and they can tell you what's out there besides trees.

# Millersburg

| | |
|---|---|
| **Number of miles:** | 15.3 |
| **Approximate pedaling time:** | 1½ hours |
| **Terrain:** | Rolling hills |
| **Surface:** | Fair |
| **Things to see:** | Small river town, agricultural valley, Susquehanna River ferry |
| **Food:** | In Millersburg |
| **Facilities:** | In community center on square in Millersburg |

Millersburg is a picturesque little town in a valley between Berry and Mahantango mountains. On a warm day, the gazebo on the square is a pleasant place to relax after an enjoyable ride.

Millersburg's greatest fame comes from Millersburg Ferry, which carries passengers across the wide Susquehanna River. It's a long way between bridges on the river, and the ferry, which uses the only remaining wooden-hulled ferryboats in the country, is both a working ferry and a tourist attraction. It's not the most impressive piece of machinery in the world, but it does its job.

The crossing takes about twenty minutes, and the biking on the other side of the river isn't good. Bicyclists can ride the ferry for $1.00, but it is seasonal, running from March until October. (For information call 717–692–2442.)

Fifteen miles east of Millersburg, the world looks entirely different as the verdant agricultural fields give way to coal seams. Pennsylvania's anthracite coal region begins about 15 miles to the east of Millersburg, but the valley through which this ride travels is entirely agricultural. One farm runs into another, and the corn grows tall.

Amish families have moved into the valley, and their presence re-

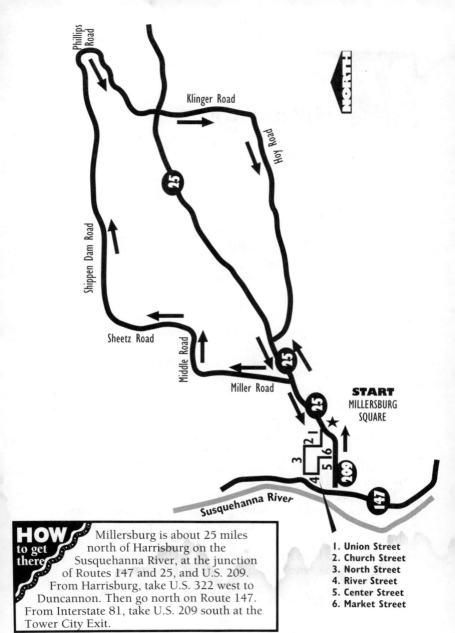

NORTH

Phillips Road

Klinger Road

Hoy Road

25

Shippen Dam Road

Sheetz Road

Middle Road

Miller Road

25

25

**START**
MILLERSBURG
SQUARE

2 1
3
4 5 6

209

147

Susquehanna River

**HOW**
to get
there

Millersburg is about 25 miles
north of Harrisburg on the
Susquehanna River, at the junction
of Routes 147 and 25, and U.S. 209.
From Harrisburg, take U.S. 322 west to
Duncannon. Then go north on Route 147.
From Interstate 81, take U.S. 209 south at the
Tower City Exit.

1. Union Street
2. Church Street
3. North Street
4. River Street
5. Center Street
6. Market Street

- Begin at the square in Millersburg, at the intersection of Route 147 and U.S. Route 209.
- Go north on U.S. 209 (Union Street).
- Left on Route 25 (Johnson Street) at 0.4 mile.
- Left on Miller Road at 1.6 miles.
- Right on Middle Road at 2.6 miles.
- Left on Sheetz Road at 2.9 miles.
- Right on Shippen Dam Road at 3.8 miles.
- Right on Phillips Road at 7.2 miles.
- Bear right on Phillips Road at 7.3 miles.
- Bear left on Phillips Road at 8.3 miles.
- Cross Route 25 to Klinger Road at 8.7 miles.
- Bear right on Klinger at 10.0 miles.
- Right on Hoy Road at 10.2 miles.
- Bear right on Hoy at 11.8 miles.
- Left on Route 25 (Berrysville Road) at 12.2 miles.
- Right on Union Street at 14.2 miles.
- Right on Church Street at 14.4 miles.
- Left on North Street at 14.5 miles.
- Left on River Street at 15.0 miles.
- Left on Center Street at 15.1 miles.
- Right on Market Street at 15.2 miles.
- Finish at 15.3 miles.

duces the number of motor vehicles on the road. The ride meanders past the base of Mahantango Mountain, through farmland and wooded areas, and past an Amish schoolhouse. Keep your eyes open for deer and other interesting wildlife on Shippen Dam Road.

Back in Millersburg, the ride takes you to the Susquehanna River and the ferry. Beside the ferry is a park where you can watch the river flow. The Susquehanna is generally a placid river, but occasionally floods with a vengeance and towns along its route have marks showing the depth of different floods.

The best time to ride is between 9:00 A.M. and 2:00 P.M; traffic picks up significantly after work and school.

# Thompsontown

|                            |                                                      |
| -------------------------- | ---------------------------------------------------- |
| **Number of miles:**       | 26.3                                                 |
| **Approximate pedaling time:** | 2¹/₂ hours                                        |
| **Terrain:**               | Almost flat                                          |
| **Surface:**               | Good                                                 |
| **Things to see:**         | Forests, farms, trains, Juniata River, small towns   |
| **Food:**                  | In Thompsontown, Port Royal, Mexico, and Mifflintown |
| **Facilities:**            | At beginning, and in towns                           |

The Juniata River is the major waterway through south-central Pennsylvania. This ride takes you for a scenic, low-traffic ride through the Juniata River Valley, on both sides of the river. By Pennsylvania standards, it's flat.

Juniata County is lightly populated, because most of the area is quite mountainous. On this ride you'll have steep hillsides looming around you, but you won't have to climb any of them. As you begin, you'll cross the Juniata River, and you'll see railroad tracks. They're the main east–west tracks for Amtrak and Conrail, so rail fans will want to bring along a camera.

Most of the first 10 miles are through a forest where wildlife is abundant. Don't be surprised to see deer, turkey vultures, bluebirds, foxes, and maybe even a bear. The latter have been moving back into the area, but they pose no threat to humans, unless the humans threaten them.

When the forest ends, you'll come into several small towns, the first of which is Port Royal. Its fame comes from its auto-racing track, which operates on weekends in warm weather. Mifflin and Mif-

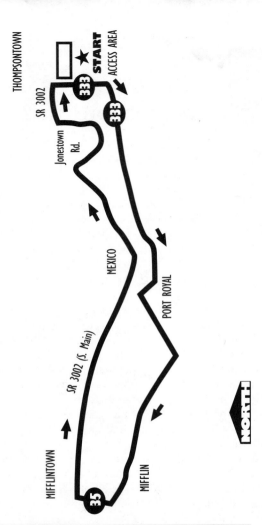

THOMPSONTOWN

START
ACCESS AREA

SR 3002

333

333

Jonestown Rd.

MEXICO

PORT ROYAL

SR 3002 (S. Main)

MIFFLINTOWN

MIFFLIN

35

NORTH

**HOW**
to get
there

Thompsontown is on U.S. Route 322, about 40 miles west of Harrisburg. Take the exit for Route 333. Follow 333 west to the Fish Commission Access beside the Juniata River.

**DIREC-TIONS for the ride**

- Leave the access area and go left, across the river.
- Follow Route 333 west through Port Royal to Mifflin.
- Take Route 35 north across the river at 14.1 miles.
- Right onto SR 3002 (South Main Street) at 14.7 miles.
- Follow road through Mexico.
- Right onto Jonestown Road at 21.0 miles.
- Right onto SR 3002 at 23.6 miles.
- Right onto Route 333 at 25.6 miles.
- Finish at 26.3 miles.

flintown are small towns on either side of the river. Mexico is an even smaller town.

After you pass Port Royal, you'll move into farm country. On the north side of the river, farms, many owned by Amish families, are quite common. Like most Pennsylvania rides, this one can be especially spectacular in October, when the leaves are changing.

# Eagles Mere

|  |  |
|---:|:---|
| Number of miles: | 14 |
| Approximate pedaling time: | 1¹/₂ hours |
| Terrain: | Very hilly |
| Surface: | Good |
| Things to see: | Resort town of Eagles Mere, Eagles Mere Lake, Sullivan County Museum (open Wednesday afternoons and Saturdays) |
| Food: | In Laporte and Eagles Mere |
| Facilities: | In Laporte and Eagles Mere |

Eagles Mere is a tiny town that's a summer home for many families. It's like a beach resort, except that it's situated on top of a mountain and it has a lake instead of an ocean.

The area surrounding Eagles Mere is known as the Endless Mountains, and the description is apt. This ride includes a couple of tough climbs and also a couple of great downhill runs.

The ride begins in Laporte, the county seat of Sullivan County, the least densely populated county in eastern Pennsylvania. In Laporte you'll find a general store, the county courthouse, a lot of trees, and a green with park benches. The road from Laporte to Eagles Mere passes through almost unbroken woodland. There are a few houses, but it's mostly trees.

On the edge of Eagles Mere is a sign that proclaims its elevation—2,126 feet. The elevation and the lake have combined to make the town a summer resort. The elevation makes Eagles Mere cooler than most parts of the state, and the lake is the focus of summer activities such as swimming and boating. In winter the lake freezes and becomes a popular spot for ice and snow activities.

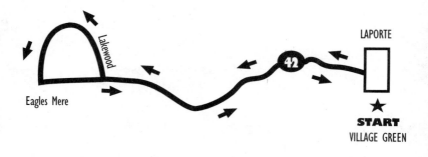

Lakewood

Eagles Mere

42

LAPORTE

★
START
VILLAGE GREEN

HOW to get there

Laporte is on U.S. Route 220, between Williamsport and Towanda. Eagles Mere is on Route 42.

**DIRECTIONS for the ride**

- Start in Laporte at the courthouse, at the intersection of Muncy and Main.
- Go south on Route 42.
- Right onto Lakewood at 5.2 miles.
- Left onto Eagles Mere Avenue (Route 42) at 7.2 miles.
- Finish at 14.0 miles.

Eagles Mere has a number of shops, which offer antiques, books, and ice cream, designed to attract tourists. It also has several inns, in case you'd like to stay overnight. On a clear day you can get a great view of the valley to the south.

Back in Laporte you can check out local history at the Sullivan County Museum, which is just behind the courthouse.

# Eckley

| | |
|---:|:---|
| **Number of miles:** | 10.1 |
| **Approximate pedaling time:** | 1 hour |
| **Terrain:** | Rolling, no tough hills |
| **Surface:** | Fair |
| **Things to see:** | Eckley Miners Village, coal-mining museum, strip mines, town of Free-land |
| **Food:** | In Freeland |
| **Facilities:** | At museum and in Freeland |

Coal was the attraction that brought thousands of European immigrants to northeastern Pennsylvania during the nineteenth and early twentieth centuries. They came to work in the mines and found jobs that were dangerous and dirty. At Eckley you can get a glimpse of life in a mining town. Movie watchers saw Eckley in *The Molly Maguires*, which was filmed here.

Eckley is a *patch* town that's less than a mile long. In its prime, the mining company owned everything: the mines, houses, stores, hotel, and schools. Underground mining operations began around 1854, and the population of Eckley peaked in 1870 at more than 1,000. Strip mining began in 1890, and the work force and general population gradually declined. That scenario has recurred across the entire region. Pennsylvania's coal production peaked in the 1920s and has been declining since because other fuels are cleaner and easier to obtain. Around Eckley, however, some mining still goes on, and you'll be able to see several strip mines as you ride.

Today, the museum at Eckley depicts the lives of coal miners in the town and across "the coal regions," which is how Pennsylvanians

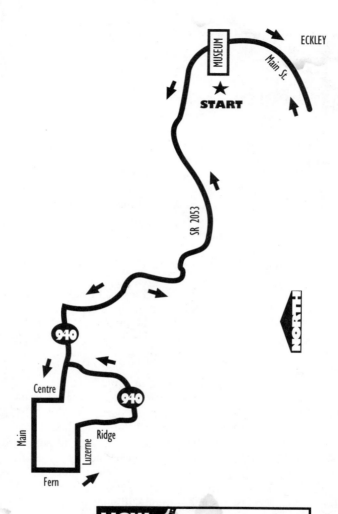

ECKLEY

Main St.

MUSEUM

★
**START**

SR 2053

940

940

Centre

Main

Ridge

Luzerne

Fern

NORTH

**HOW** to get there   Take Route 940 east from Hazelton or west from Interstate 80 and follow signs for Eckley Miners Village.

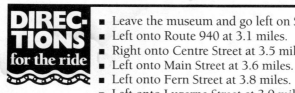

**DIRECTIONS for the ride**

- Leave the museum and go left on SR 2053.
- Left onto Route 940 at 3.1 miles.
- Right onto Centre Street at 3.5 miles.
- Left onto Main Street at 3.6 miles.
- Left onto Fern Street at 3.8 miles.
- Left onto Luzerne Street at 3.9 miles.
- Right onto Ridge Street at 4.0 miles.
- Left at T intersection (Route 940) at 4.3 miles.
- Right onto Route 940 at 4.6 miles.
- Right onto SR 2053 at 5.1 miles.
- Right into museum at 8.3 miles.

**Note:** The village is about .9 mile long. If you ride to the end and back, you'll have traveled 10.1 miles.

refer to a large area of their state. In fact, Pennsylvania produces two different types of coal. Bituminous, or soft coal, is more common. Anthracite, which comes out of the ground at Eckley, is harder, and it burns more cleanly.

The ride begins at the museum and goes to the small town of Freeland. The entire area sits on top of a mountain, so there are no especially strenuous climbs. Along the route you can see coal mines that are still operating. You'll also see some amazing sights where grass and trees have somehow managed to grow in the residue left from the mining and refining processes.

WELCOME TO
HARVEYS LAKE
LARGEST NATURAL LAKE IN
PENNSYLVANIA
HARVEYS LAKE LIONS CLUB

# Harveys Lake

| | |
|---:|:---|
| **Number of miles:** | 11.5 |
| **Approximate pedaling time:** | 1 hour |
| **Terrain:** | Flat for 8.3 miles, with an option for 3.2 miles of hills |
| **Surface:** | Good |
| **Things to see:** | Lake and beautiful homes |
| **Food:** | Numerous places |
| **Facilities:** | At beginning and at restaurants |

Harveys Lake is the largest natural lake within Pennsylvania's borders, and it provides a totally flat 8.3-mile ride. If you like hills, you can go away from the lake in any direction and know that you'll do some good climbing, but if you like flat and scenic rides, you can do loops around the lake.

Harveys Lake lies about 12 miles northwest of Wilkes-Barre, in a highly industrialized region known for coal mining. In the region around the lake, however, recreation is the main industry, and the steep hills surrounding the lake seem to block out the rest of the world and its hurried pace and its problems.

Harveys Lake is also the name of the town around the lake and the region has the relaxed atmosphere of a resort. Ringing the lake are many large and beautiful homes, and the lake itself is a favorite recreational spot. Boats are plentiful, and bikers and runners enjoy the flat road around the lake, especially on weekends. This is one ride that's probably better on weekdays, because the traffic is much lighter then.

The ride begins at the Pennsylvania Fish Commission facility on the western side of the lake and follows the road around the

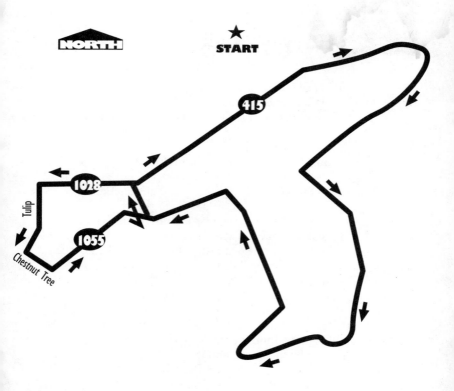

NORTH

★
**START**

**415**

**1028**

Tulip

**1055**

Chestnut Tree

**HOW** to get there
Take Interstate 81 to Wilkes-Barre. Go north on 309. In Dallas, take 415 and follow signs to Harveys Lake.

**DIREC-TIONS**
**for the ride**

- Begin at Pennsylvania Fish Commission boat launch area on west side of lake.
- Leave the parking lot and go right, following the road around the lake for 8.3 miles.
- For a little climbing after the loop:
- Left on SR 1028 at 8.4 miles.
- Left on Tulip Road (SR 1065) at 9.7 miles.
- Left on Chestnut Tree Road at 10.3 miles.
- Left on SR 1055 at 10.4 miles.
- Right on SR 415 and finish at 11.5 miles.

water. Restaurants and recreational facilities, including boat rentals, are at the southern end of the lake, about 5 miles into the ride. You'll go in circles here, and you'll find the circles quite pleasant.

# Honesdale

| | |
|---:|:---|
| **Number of miles:** | 11.7 |
| **Approximate pedaling time:** | 1 hour |
| **Terrain:** | Hilly |
| **Surface:** | Fair |
| **Things to see:** | America's first railroad, Wayne County fairgrounds, Wayne County Museum |
| **Food:** | In Honesdale |
| **Facilities:** | In Honesdale |

Honesdale is a pretty little town in the Pocono Mountains of Wayne County. It lies in a basin, surrounded on all sides by fairly steep hills, and, although it's the biggest town in the county, it's definitely a small town. The village green, across from the courthouse, is a pleasant place to sit and relax after your ride.

In 1829 Honesdale became the site of the first trip by steam locomotive in the United States, when the Stourbridge Lion made its initial journey. Imported from England to haul coal from nearby mines to the Delaware and Hudson Canal, it proved too heavy for the rails. Despite that early disappointment, trains played a big part in Honesdale's growth. Today, the town's rail heritage is still strong. During the summer and fall, and near holidays such as Easter, Halloween, and Christmas, weekend excursion trains run from Honesdale to Hawley and Lackawaxen.

If your travel around Pennsylvania, you'll observe that, to a considerable extent, Wayne County reverses traditional land-use patterns. In many places farms are in the valleys, whereas the higher areas remain unpopulated. In Wayne County, however, many farms are on the tops of hills, and the lowlands are home to the area's towns.

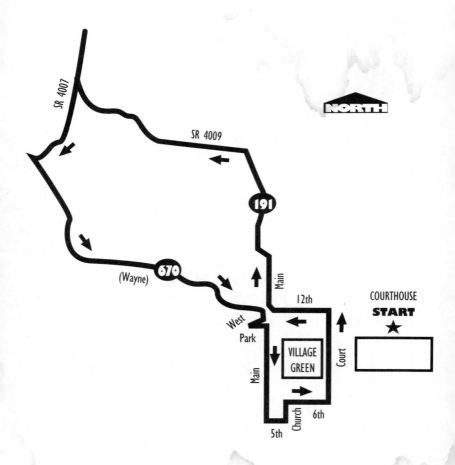

SR 4007

SR 4009

NORTH

191

(Wayne) 670

Main

12th

West

Park

Main

VILLAGE
GREEN

Court

COURTHOUSE
**START**
★

Church 6th

5th

**HOW** to get there    Honesdale is in the northeastern corner of Pennsylvania, at the intersection of U.S. Route 6, Route 191, and Route 670. From Interstate 84, take Route 191 north. From Interstate 81, take U.S. Route 6 east.

- Begin at the Wayne County Court House, two blocks east of Main Street, and go north on Court Street.
- Left onto Twelfth Street at 0.2 mile.
- Right onto Main Street at 0.3 mile.
- North onto Route 191.
- Left onto SR 4009 at 4.2 miles.
- Left onto SR 4007 at 5.7 miles.
- Left onto Wayne Street (Route 670) at 6.9 miles.
- Right onto Main Street at 9.9 miles.
- Right onto West Street at 10.1 miles.
- Left onto Park Street at 10.5 miles.
- Right onto Main Street at 10.6 miles.
- Train rides are at 10.8 miles.
- Left onto Fifth Street at 11.2 miles.
- Left onto Church Street at 11.3 miles.
- Right onto Sixth Street at 11.35 miles.
- Left onto Court Street at 11.4 miles.
- Finish at 11.7 miles.

Agriculture and logging are both important here, and they're on display at the Wayne County Fair. It takes place in early August at the fairgrounds on Route 191, about 1.5 miles into the ride.

# Jim Thorpe–Lehigh Gorge State Park Trail

| | |
|---:|:---|
| **Number of miles:** | 44 round trip |
| **Approximate pedaling time:** | 4 hours |
| **Terrain:** | Basically flat, with upgrade from Jim Thorpe to White Haven |
| **Surface:** | Good, with some rough spots |
| **Things to see:** | White-water river, nature, flaming foliage in autumn, waterfalls, trains |
| **Food:** | In Jim Thorpe and White Haven |
| **Facilities:** | At both ends and in middle of trail |

The Lehigh Gorge is steep and access is difficult. No roads cross the river for 19 miles. Building the railroad was a difficult engineering feat, and you'll see evidence of the blasting that was necessary.

For the first 6 miles, the trail runs beside the tracks of the Reading and Northern, a short-line railroad that still uses the tracks. About 6 miles north of Jim Thorpe, the rail lines branch off. One branch crosses the river and runs along the other side. Another branch goes west. From that point north, the trail no longer runs beside the tracks.

The best part of the trail is the opportunity that it offers to ride with no interference from cars. It's actually 19.6 miles to the only road crossing along the entire route, but traffic of a different kind is still present. The trail is popular with hikers and bikers, and most of them move rather slowly.

Waterfalls are one of the scenic delights along the route. The walls of the gorge rise very steeply, and some waterfalls are almost direct

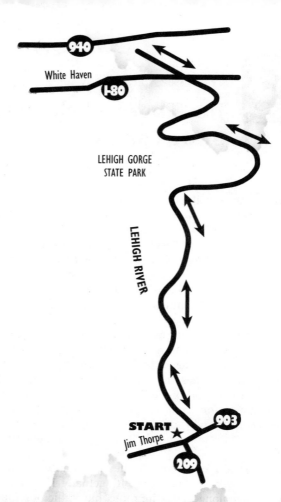

**HOW** to get there — Jim Thorpe is in northeastern Pennsylvania, at the intersection of U.S. Route 209 and 903. To reach Jim Thorpe take the northeast extension of the Pennsylvania Turnpike to the Lehighton exit and go south on U.S. 209, which will take you to Jim Thorpe. From downtown Jim Thorpe, follow 209 south. Cross the Lehigh River on the 903 bridge. Stay on 903 for 3 blocks. Come to a STOP sign and stop. Go down hill and follow road for about one-half mile. Take first left (at Jim Thorpe River Adventures), follow road to parking area.

**DIREC-
TIONS
for the ride**

- The trail begins where the parking area ends. Go north. It's the only way you can go.

verticals. Birds, squirrels, and deer are plentiful, and some trail users have seen bears.

The trail rises 589 feet from Jim Thorpe to White Haven, and that drop makes the return ride easier. It also makes the Lehigh River one of the better white-water rafting streams in Pennsylvania. If you ride when the water is high, generally in spring, you can see rafters on the river.

At the northern end of the trail is the town of White Haven. The rail ends in the parking lot of The White Haven Shopping Center. A supermarket is in the shopping center and several restaurants are on nearby streets. If you feel a need to ride over a few hills, just ride around White Haven.

The most scenic time to do this ride is early October, when the leaves are at their most brilliant. They turn spectacular shades of red and gold during the first two weeks of the month.

Jim Thorpe has become an artsy little tourist town. Galleries and antiques shops line the streets, and the tourist center in the railroad station has all the information you may need, including information on the trail.

Jim Thorpe draws big crowds when the weather is good, and parking downtown can be tough, so if you don't mind a few more miles and a few hills, it's a good idea to leave the car at the trail and ride to downtown.

# Athens

| | |
|---:|:---|
| Number of miles: | 10.1 |
| Approximate pedaling time: | 1 hour |
| Terrain: | Flat |
| Surface: | Good |
| Things to see: | Tioga Point Museum, Valley Railroad Museum |
| Food: | Numerous places along route |
| Facilities: | At Tioga Point Museum and all along route |

Tucked between the Chemung and Susquehanna rivers, just south of the New York border, is one of the few large expanses of flat land in northeastern Pennsylvania. This short ride will take you through the pleasant small towns of Athens and Sayre that occupy much of that land. At this point the Susquehanna is still a young and growing river, and it's quite narrow, at least in comparison to the width of a mile that it reaches in southern Pennsylvania.

The ride begins at the southern end of Athens and meanders through the two towns. Tioga Point was an Indian settlement, and at the Tioga Point Museum, you can learn much of the history of the region. A part of that history was composer Stephen Foster, who wrote some of his early works here. In fact, the Camptown of the song "De Camptown Races" lies about 25 miles southeast of Athens.

Three miles into the ride, you can stop at the Valley Railroad Museum in downtown Sayre and learn about the trains that made Sayre a bustling railroad town. Some freight trains still run, but their frequency is down substantially from half a century ago.

The rest of the ride is a leisurely trek through business and residential areas. You'll pass parks and open spaces that invite you to stop, relax, and look at the mountains that rise up in all direc-

**DIREC-TIONS for the ride**

- Begin at Tioga Point Museum, 724 South Main Street.
- From the Tioga Point Museum, go north on Main Street.
- Main Street becomes Keystone Avenue.
- Right on West Lockhart at 2.3 miles.
- Right on North Elmer Street at 2.8 miles.
- Left on West Parker Street at 2.9 miles.
- Left on Desmond Street at 3.0 miles.
- Valley Railroad Museum is on left.
- At intersection of Desmond and Lockhart, bear left on Desmond, parallel to railroad tracks.
- Desmond becomes North Lehigh Avenue.
- Left on Bradford Street at 4.3 miles.
- Right on North Wilbur Street at 4.5 miles.
- Left on Henry Street at 4.7 miles.
- Left on Warren Street at 4.8 miles.
- Right on Pitney Street at 5.1 miles.
- Left on Elmira Street at 5.9 miles.
- Left on West Lockhart Avenue at 6.6 miles.
- Right on Pennsylvania Avenue at 7.1 miles.
- Left on Pine Street at 8.3 miles.
- Right on Main Street at 8.7 miles.
- Left on Susquehanna Street at 9.5 miles.
- Right on Edward Street at 9.6 miles.*
- Left on South Main Street at 9.8 miles.
- Finish at 10.1 miles.

*If you're interested in a spectacular view, and you like *arduous* climbs, cross the bridge, go to the four-way intersection and turn right. Then take the first left and climb. When you get to the top, you'll have a view of a beautiful valley.

tions. In autumn, you can admire the fire on the surrounding mountains as the leaves turn to brilliant shades of red and gold.

Warren
Henry
N. Wilbur
Pitney
Bradford
NORTH
Elmira
209
N. Lehigh
Desmond
W. Lockhart
N. Elmer
W. Parker
Pennsylvania
Keystone
CHEMUNG
SUSQUEHANNA RIVER
Pine
Susquehanna St.
Edward St.
Main
★ START
TIOGA PT.
MUSEUM

**HOW to get there** Take U.S. Route 220 to the northern reaches of Pennsylvania. Just south of Athens, take 199 north to Main Street in Athens. Tioga Point Museum is at 724 South Main Street.

# Canton

| | |
|---|---|
| **Number of miles:** | 31 |
| **Approximate pedaling time:** | 3 hours |
| **Terrain:** | Hilly |
| **Surface:** | Good |
| **Things to see:** | Farms and forests, valley views |
| **Food:** | Few opportunities: tavern at 15 miles, general store at 23 miles |
| **Facilities:** | At tavern |

This is a fairly long and challenging ride, but by local standards, it's practically flat. The ride will take you on both sides of the valley formed by Towanda Creek. Farming dominates the valley and mountains are always nearby. This course will allow you to pedal for a long time with just a few turns.

The two major attractions on this jaunt are the long, straight stretches and the scenery. A mile and a half into the ride, you may want to stop and enjoy the view of the valley. If you can ride in late September or early October, the leaves will welcome you with dazzling shades of red and gold.

A third attraction is the lack of traffic on all the roads, with the exception of the short stretch of Route 414. Basically, this is a place to ride and enjoy the serenity of a beautiful rural area. The two potential places to stop for food are the Granville Tavern, on Route 514 about 15 miles into the ride, and a general store/post office near the 23-mile mark.

When you turn left onto Cowley Road at 22.5 miles, notice the abandoned wooden railroad bridge. The trains are gone now, but when they ran, this was close to the highest point on the line. It

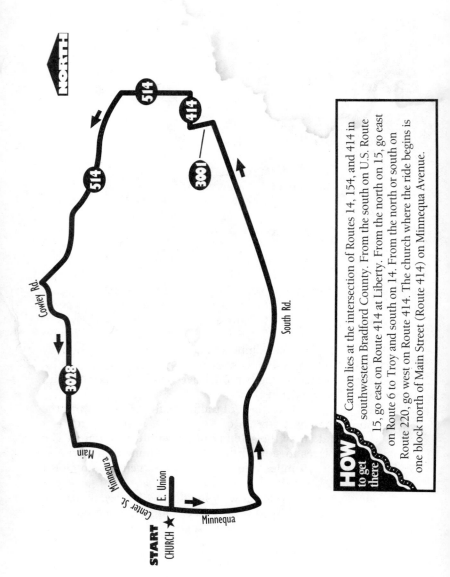

NORTH

514
514
414
3001

Cowley Rd.

3028

Main
Center St.
Minnequa Ave.

START
CHURCH ★

E. Union

Minnequa

South Rd.

**HOW to get there**

Canton lies at the intersection of Routes 14, 154, and 414 in southwestern Bradford County. From the south on U.S. Route 15, go east on Route 414 at Liberty. From the north on 15, go east on Route 6 to Troy and south on 14. From the north or south on Route 220, go west on Route 414. The church where the ride begins is one block north of Main Street (Route 414) on Minnequa Avenue.

- Begin at church parking lot at corner of Union Street and Minnequa Avenue.
- Start out by going south (downhill) on Minnequa.
- Left on South Road at 0.5 mile.
- Left on SR 3001 at 13.2 miles.
- Right on Route 414 at 13.5 miles.
- Left on Route 514 at 13.8 miles.
- Left on Cowley Road (SR 3028) at 22.5 miles.
- Bend to the left at 23 miles (store and post office are here).
- Right on SR 3028 at 23.7 miles.
- Left on Minnequa Main at 26.2 miles.
- Bend to right at 28.1 miles.
- Becomes Center Street in Canton.
- Left on East Union Street at 30.8 miles.
- Finish at 31 miles.

was a route that must have required all the power that engines could muster to get over these hills. From this point in the ride, you can frequently see the old railroad grade as you head into Canton. You can also enjoy knowing that it's mostly downhill for the rest of the ride.

**Note:** On this ride, more than any other, the author encountered dogs running loose. It's always a good idea to carry a spray to deter dogs.

# Loganton/Sugar Valley

| | |
|---:|:---|
| **Number of miles:** | 15.4 |
| **Approximate pedaling time:** | 1½ hours |
| **Terrain:** | Almost flat |
| **Surface:** | Good |
| **Things to see:** | Small town, covered bridge, fertile valley |
| **Food:** | In Loganton |
| **Facilities:** | In Loganton |

The dictionary defines a valley as "a stretch of low land lying between hills or mountains and usually having a stream or river flowing through it." Sugar Valley fits that definition perfectly.

Sugar Valley is about 1 mile wide and 10 miles long. It lies just south of Interstate 80, but most of the traffic zooms by, never stopping to investigate what lies nearby.

Steep hillsides rise on both sides of the valley. Fishing Creek runs right down the middle, and most of the land in the valley is farmed. For a bicyclist it's a great place to take a leisurely ride. There are only a few roads in the valley, but they don't have much traffic on them. And many residents of the valley are Amish farmers, who use buggies instead of cars.

Loganton is a picturesque, small town. It's home to the valley's schools and a few businesses. Once you get out of town, you're immediately in farm country. On Logan's Mill Road you'll pass through Logan's Mill Bridge, the only covered bridge left in Clinton County. After a short climb away from the water, you'll be on the south side of the valley. From there you'll have an excellent view of the valley's farms and orchards.

LOGANTON
**START**

880

Snook

880

477

Logan's Mill

SR 2002

NORTH

**HOW** to get there

Loganton lies just south of Interstate 80, about 30 miles west of the Susquehanna River. Follow the signs for Route 880.

**DIREC-
TIONS
for the ride**

- Begin in the center of Loganton, at the intersection of Routes 880 and 477.
- Go south on 880.
- Left onto Logan's Mill Road at 5.5 miles.
- Left onto SR 2002 at 6.4 miles.
- Left onto Snook Road at 11.8 miles.
- Left onto Route 880 at 12.7 miles.
- Finish at 15.4 miles.

As rides go, this is short on tourist attractions but long on scenery and enjoyable riding.

# Penn's Creek

|  |  |
|--:|:--|
| Number of miles: | 17 |
| Approximate pedaling time: | 1½ hours |
| Terrain: | Rolling |
| Surface: | Mostly good; one bad stretch on School Road |
| Things to see: | Walnut Acres Organic Farm, rolling farmlands, Buggy Museum |
| Food: | At Walnut Acres and in Mifflinburg and New Berlin |
| Facilities: | At Walnut Acres and in Mifflinburg and New Berlin |

This pleasant jaunt will take you through the fertile farmland of Union and Snyder counties. Beginning at Walnut Acres Farm, you'll pass farm after farm and go through two small towns.

Walnut Acres Farm was one of the first in the country to make the break from chemical farming. In 1946, long before organic foods gained the popularity that they have today, Paul Keene decided to grow his crops without applying harmful chemicals to the land. Today, Mr. Keene is still active in his business, and Walnut Acres is a big food company. (Well, big by the standards of its industry, although still small in comparison to a company such as Kraft or Hershey.)

At Walnut Acres you'll find a retail store and a small restaurant. Actually, a very small percentage of the Walnut Acres sales comes from this store. Most of their sales come through natural-food stores and mail order. You can also take plant tours. If you're really lucky, you'll get there on a day when they're roasting peanuts and making peanut butter.

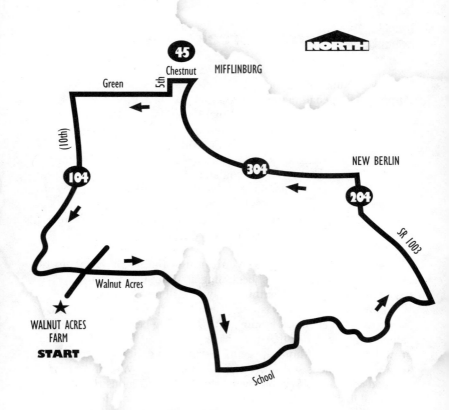

**NORTH**

45 Chestnut **MIFFLINBURG**

Green 5th

(10th)

104

304 **NEW BERLIN**

204

SR 1003

Walnut Acres

★
**WALNUT ACRES
FARM**

**START**

School

**HOW to get there** From Harrisburg, take U.S. Route 15 north to Route 104 north. Go about 20 miles and look for the signs for Walnut Acres; the ride begins at Walnut Acres Farm. From Lewisburg, take Route 45 west to Route 104 south and look for the Walnut Acres signs.

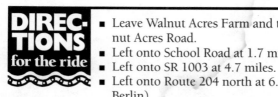

**DIRECTIONS for the ride**

- Leave Walnut Acres Farm and turn right on Walnut Acres Road.
- Left onto School Road at 1.7 miles.
- Left onto SR 1003 at 4.7 miles.
- Left onto Route 204 north at 6.3 miles (New Berlin).
- Left onto Chestnut Street (Route 45 west) at 12.1 miles (Mifflinburg).
- Left onto Fifth Street at 12.2 miles.
- Right onto Green Street at 12.3 miles.
- Left onto Tenth Street (Route 104 south) at 12.8 miles.
- Left onto Walnut Acres Road at 16.4 miles.
- Right into Walnut Acres Farm at 17.0 miles.

When you head out on the roads, you'll be in farm country. The first town that you'll reach is New Berlin, a quiet town with a nice little park right beside the creek.

Five miles down the road from New Berlin, you'll come to Mifflinburg, the biggest town on the ride. Mifflinburg offers several places of interest. One is the Buggy Museum on Green Street. At one time, Mifflinburg was the carriage-making center of the world. The museum remembers those days. And on Chestnut Street you'll find a shop that features quilts made by the Amish and Mennonite ladies of the area.

# Wellsboro–Pine Creek Trail

| | |
|---:|:---|
| **Number of miles:** | 19 each way |
| **Approximate pedaling time:** | 4 hours |
| **Terrain:** | Flat |
| **Surface:** | Good |
| **Things to see:** | Nature, wildlife, white-water stream |
| **Food:** | At hotel in Blackwell |
| **Facilities:** | At ends of trail and at campground in middle |

Pennsylvania's Grand Canyon is less famous and more beautiful than some big hole in the ground out west. Fifty miles long and, in places, 1,000 feet deep, Pennsylvania's Grand Canyon is a green gorge cut by Pine Creek through the mountains of northern Pennsylvania.

The Pine Creek Trail has given a new use to an abandoned railroad right-of-way, and in the process it has opened the floor of the canyon to the public for the first time. When the railroad was running, the public had very little opportunity to travel through the canyon. The gorge is narrow, and the railroad bed was the only road through it. Now, hikers and bikers can travel through the canyon, enjoy nature, and forget about cars.

Eventually, this trail will be 62 miles long, stretching from Wellsboro Junction to Jersey Shore. Currently it's 19 miles of superb and easy biking with only one road crossing.

This definitely is a leisurely ride. The surface is gravel, and it's fine for either road or mountain bikes. Deer frequently wander onto the trail, and when the water is deep enough, white-water rafters fill the creek. The trail is downhill from Ansonia to Blackwell, but the grade

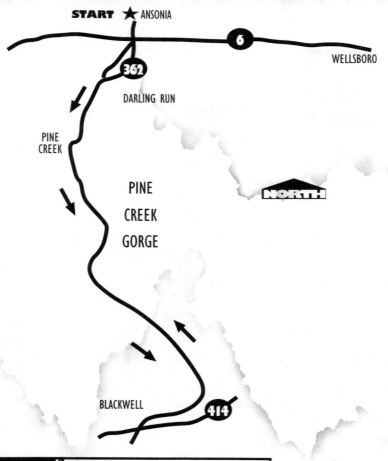

START ★ ANSONIA

6 WELLSBORO

362

DARLING RUN

PINE CREEK

PINE CREEK GORGE

NORTH

BLACKWELL

414

**HOW to get there** Wellsboro is in Tioga County in north-central Pennsylvania, just south of the New York border. The Pine Creek Trail begins in Ansonia, which is on U.S. Route 6, 10 miles west of Wellsboro. The parking area lies just west of Pine Creek. Coming from Wellsboro, cross the bridge across the creek and turn right. The parking area is straight ahead. Another parking area is at Darling Run. Coming from Wellsboro, turn left on Route 362 and go 1 miles to the Darling Run access.

■ Enjoy the ride.

is negligible.

Through most of the canyon, things look much as they did a hundred years ago. The canyon walls are too steep to permit any sort of development, and only a few houses are visible along the entire route. Blackwell is a small town near the southern end of the trail, and locals say that the food is good at the hotel. It's a better idea, however, to carry supplies with you. The only other source of food is abundant wild berries that ripen in late summer.

Above all, this is an ideal ride when you just want to avoid dealing with cars. Dress warmly. Even in summer, mornings an be cool until the sun climbs above the rim of the canyon.

The town of Wellsboro, 10 miles east, is an excellent place to stay while you explore the region. In addition to the trail, you'll find a tourist railroad, a beautiful old hotel, a town green, several lakes, and the State Laurel Festival in June. To rent bikes, call Pine Creek Outfitters in Ansonia (717–724–3003).

# Washingtonville

|                           |                                           |
| ------------------------- | ----------------------------------------- |
| **Number of miles:**      | 19                                        |
| **Approximate pedaling time:** | 1½ hours                             |
| **Terrain:**              | Flat, one hill                            |
| **Surface:**              | Good                                      |
| **Things to see:**        | Montour Preserve, fertile farmlands       |
| **Food:**                 | In Washingtonville, store at 8.4 miles    |
| **Facilities:**           | At Montour Preserve                       |

This ride is amazingly flat. In 19 miles there is only one hill. It's also a very pretty ride, meandering through some of the best farmland in north-central Pennsylvania.

The ride begins at the Montour Preserve. The preserve, maintained by the Pennsylvania Power and Light Company (PP&L), is a great place to see nature at work. It offers picnic areas, Lake Chillisquaque for boating, and hiking trails, Wildlife Management areas, and even a fossil pit where you can dig and keep whatever you find.

The Laura Smith Trail of History will take you through the preserve. If you follow this trail, you can see old farmhouses, farm tools, barns, and the little Chillisquaque Creek.

Leaving the preserve, you'll ride out into the farm country of Montour County. On the roads you'll probably see some Amish horses and buggies. The ride goes through a lush valley, nestled between the Muncy Hills to the north and the Montour Ridge to the south. You'll see steep hills looming around you, but except for the little climb at 8.5 miles, you won't have to go up any of them. The major town on the ride is Washingtonville, a quiet little farming community.

You'll see two big towers as you ride. They are part of the Montour Steam Electric Station, a coal-fired generating plant operated by PP&L to supply electricity for Pennsylvania.

**163**

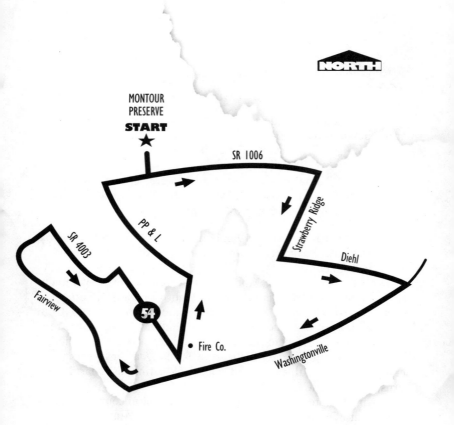

**NORTH**

MONTOUR
PRESERVE
**START**
★

SR 1006

PP & L

Strawberry Ridge

Diehl

SR 4003

Fairview

**54**

• Fire Co.

Washingtonville

**HOW** to get there The Montour Preserve, where your ride begins, lies close to Route 54 in Montour County, north of Interstate 80 and Washingtonville. Get off Interstate 80 at Exit 33 and go north on Route 54. The signs will direct you to the preserve.

- Leave the parking lot at the Montour Preserve and go left on SR 1006.
- Right onto Strawberry Ridge Road (SR 1002) at 1.7 miles.
- Left onto Diehl Road at 3.7 miles.
- Right onto Washingtonville Road at 5.2 miles.
- Right onto Fairview Road at 8.4 miles.
- Right onto SR 4003 at 11.2 miles (stop sign).
- Right onto Route 54 at 12.3 miles.
- Left onto unmarked road at 15.0 miles. Look for signs to Montour Preserve and Washingtonville Volunteer Fire Company.
- Left onto PP&L Road at 16.0 miles.
- Left into Preserve at 19.2 miles.

Notice the farms in this valley. PP&L owns some of them and leases them to local farmers, stipulating that they employ modern farming practices such as crop rotation, contour farming, and erosion control. The results of excellent land management are increased yields and better soil fertility. In this verdant valley man and nature do a great job of getting along.

# Mountoursville/Williamsport

| | |
|---:|:---|
| **Number of miles:** | 14.1 each way |
| **Approximate pedaling time:** | 3 hours |
| **Terrain:** | Mostly flat |
| **Surface:** | Good |
| **Things to see:** | Parks, creek, Susquehanna River, Lycoming College |
| **Food:** | At Mountoursville and Williamsport |
| **Facilities:** | At parks at both ends of trail |

Both ends of this ride are dedicated bike paths. In the middle is a bike route that follows lightly traveled streets, a highway overpass, and trails through parks. It's a good example of what municipalities can do to make bicycle commuting a viable method of transportation. Someone living in suburban Montoursville can ride all the way to downtown Williamsport with little interference from motor vehicles.

This trail is ideal for families and everyone who likes a leisurely ride. Beginning in Indian Park in Montoursville, the trail goes through the park and a natural area. Then it runs beside the Susquehanna River before going onto residential streets in Williamsport. On the west end of the city is another bike path that runs beside Lycoming Creek.

You can stop and watch the West Branch of the Susquehanna River, which is actually a different river from the one that passes Wilkes-Barre. The two branches join near Sunbury, and Williamsport is the largest city on the West Branch. Beside the river are railroad

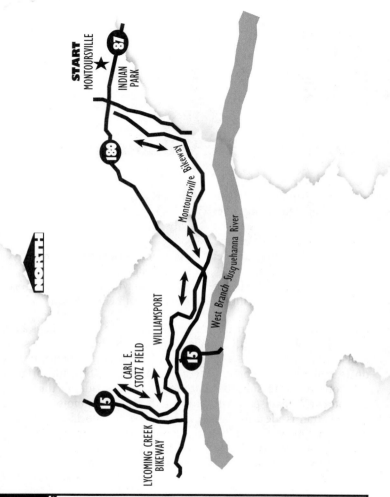

**NORTH**

START
MONTOURSVILLE
★

INDIAN PARK

87

180

Montoursville Bikeway

WILLIAMSPORT

15

CARL E. STOTZ FIELD

15

LYCOMING CREEK BIKEWAY

West Branch Susquehanna River

**HOW to get there** Lycoming County is in the center of Pennsylvania, where the West Branch of the Susquehanna River makes a big bend. The Montoursville end of the trail is the easier to find. From Interstate 180, exit at Route 87. Go south on 87 (Loyalstock Avenue) for 1/2 mile. Turn right into Indian Park. In the park turn right at the first stop sign, and that road will carry you to the trail. Or You can begin at the Wendy's on Route 87. You'll see the end of the trail in the Wendy's parking lot.

## DIREC-TIONS for the ride

- From Mountoursville follow the trail toward Williamsport. It alternates between a dedicated bike trail and a marked bike trail on lightly traveled roads and city streets. Follow the signs and they'll lead you to the Lycoming Creek Bikeway on the western side of Williamsport.

tracks, and the freight line is fairly busy.

The lumber industry brought great wealth to Williamsport, and its high school sports teams are The Millionaires. Today Williamsport is a manufacturing center whose greatest fame comes from the Little League World Series, which takes place here every August. Actually the Little League Museum and stadium are in South Williamsport, across the river on U.S. Route 15. At the end of this ride, on the Lycoming Creek Bikeway, is Carl E. Stotz Field, named after the founder of Little League.

The region is quite hilly, but this trail is primarily flat. From the path in Williamsport you can see the downtown business district, but the path stays on lightly traveled residential streets.

Indian Park is a large recreational area with open fields and many types of facilities. It's a good place to relax after the ride.

# Cross-State Bike Tours

July            ALA Bike H.O.P., Cross Pennsylvania from Pitts-
                burgh to Philadelphia. Benefits American Lung
                Association, 6041 Linglestown Road,
                Harrisburg 17112, (717) 540–8506

July            Pedal Pennsylvania, Cross Pennsylvania from
                Pittsburgh to Philadelphia, 450+ miles. 1914
                Brandywine Street, Philadelphia 19130, (215)
                561–9679

August          Perimeter Ride Against Cancer. Ride changes
                yearly; call for details. Benefits Lehigh Valley
                Unit, American Cancer Society. 500+ miles. 331
                North 22nd Street, Allentown 18104, (610)
                433–4397

# Regional Bike Tours

May–October     Inn to Inn Bicycle Tour. Five-day, self-guided
                mountain bike tour on country roads and aban-
                doned railroad beds. Accommodations at local
                B&Bs. $335 per person (plus tax) includes all
                lodging, meals, and equipment shuttles.
                Pass Realty, R.R. 1, Box 79, Uniondale 18470,
                (717) 798–2519

May             Pinch Pond Mountain Bike Weekend. Weekend
                of fun mountain bike rides and races sponsored
                by Team Gretna. 1111 Walnut Street, Lebanon
                17042, (717) 273–9499 or (717) 665–9605

                Tour de Y. Metric century, with half century option, to benefit YMCA. Start at Optimist Park, Lebanon. "Tandem-friendly" route. Lebanon Valley Bike Club, 124 West Church Street, Annville 17003, (717) 865–3833

Horse Farm Tour. Rides of 10–50 miles on flat to rolling terrain from South Street Park, McSherrystown. Hanover Cyclers, 132 Farm View Drive, York 17404, (717) 225–7184

Freedom Tour. Routes of 8, 18, 35, and 65 miles from Ridley Club, P.O. Box 274, Drexel Hill 19026, (610) 259–3327

Mexican Metric Century. Routes of 25, 35, and 63 miles from Lower Perkiomen Valley Park. Flat to moderately hilly terrain. Mexican fiesta following the ride! Suburban Cyclists Unlimited, P.O. Box 401, Horsham 19044, (215) 675–8167

John Pixton Memorial Poker Ride. Routes of 20, 30, 50, and 62 miles from Montgomery County Community College. Riders collect playing cards during ride and submit at finish for prizes. Pennsylvania Bicycle Club, P.O. Box 987, Glenside 19038, (215) 885–5128

**June**

Kutztown and Millersville Eastern Loop. 190 miles of rolling to very hilly terrain. No sag! Harrisburg Bike Club, 1554 Locust Street, New Cumberland 17070, (717) 561–1647

Blue & Gray Weekend Rally. Routes of 40–65 miles through rural Gettysburg. Maps and trip leaders provided by Bike Fed of Pennsylvania, P.O. Box 11625, Harrisburg 17108, (717) 975–0888

**July**        Tour de Lebanon Valley. Metric and half century from Annville/Cleona High School. Lebanon Valley Bicycle Club, 124 West Church Street, Annville 17003, (717) 865–3833

PNC Bank/MS Bike Tour. Two-day, 150-mile ride to raise money for Multiple Sclerosis Society. Pledges required. National MS Society, 200 Forest Hills Drive, Harrisburg 17112, (717) 652–2108

Ride the Allegheny Mountains of Pennsylvania. Circle tour of north-central Pennsylvania. 400–450 miles. RAMP 95, P.O. Box 68, Lock Haven 17745, (717) 748–5782

Tour of northeast Pennsylvania. Rolling to hilly terrain, triple chain rings recommended. 65+ miles/day. Cycle Pennsylvania, 205 Frederick Street, Moosic 18507, (717) 457–1154

**August**     Covered Bridge Tour. Two-day, 85-mile tour near Bloomsburg. Joe Donovan, 205 Frederick Road, Moosic 18507, (717) 457–1154

Grotto Pizza Great 100. 25-, 50-, and 100-mile routes on rolling to moderately hilly terrain. Wyoming Valley Bicycle Club, 428 North Maple Street, Kingston 18704, (717) 829–7226

Covered Bridge Metric Century. Full, half, and quarter metrics through scenic Lancaster County. Lancaster Bicycle Club, P.O. Box 535, Lancaster 17608, (717) 396–9299.

| September | Labor Day Century. Routes of 25, 50, 62, and 100 miles from South Street Park, McSherrystown. Flat to rolling! Hanover Cyclers, 529 Lake Meade, East Berlin 17316, (717) 259–7387 |
|---|---|
| | No Baloney Century. Routes of 25, 50, 75, and 100 miles from South Hills Park, Lebanon. Lebanon Valley Bicycle Club, 124 West Church Street, Annville 17003, (717) 865–3833 |
| | Savage Century. Generally regarded as one of the most difficult centuries on the East Coast through the worst hills in Lancaster and Chester counties! White Clay Bicycle Club, 321 Indian Town Road, Landenburg 19350, (610) 255–0799 |
| | Sid Lustig Memorial Century. Annual event by Harrisburg Bike Club, 345 Old York Road, New Cumberland 17070, (717) 975–9879 |
| | Annual Brandywine Tour. Routes of 20, 50, and 100 miles from Chadds Ford School, U.S. Route 1. Delaware Valley Bicycle Club, P.O. Box 274, Drexel Hill 19026, (215) 259–3327 |
| | Lake Nockamixon Century. Routes of 20, 35, 50, 62, and 100 miles, and 23-mile mountain bike course. Start at Hatboro-Horsham High School. Flat to moderately hilly terrain. Suburban Cyclists Unlimited, P.O. Box 401, Horsham 19044, (215) 675–8167 |
| October | Covered Bridge Fall Classic Bicycle Race. 75-mile USCF-sanctioned race crossing fifteen covered |

bridges. Columbia–Montour TPA, 121 Papermill Road, Bloomsburg 17815, (800) VISIT–10

Spring Mountain Bike Races. Mountain bike races sponsored by Bikesport, 371 Main Street, Harleysville 19438, (215) 256–6613

## Bike Shops

(Shops, listed alphabetically by city or town, sell and service bikes and provide maps or other touring information. Shops designated by an * also provide rentals.)
Lebanon Valley Bike Club

*Bike Line
1728 Tilghman Street
Allentown 18104
(610) 439–1724

McFarland Bike Shop
15 North Main Street
Ambler 19002
(215) 646–2843

Bonner's Cycle
R.D. 1, Box 534
Avis 17721
(717) 753–5702

Bike Line
2112 Shoenersville Road
Bethlehem 18013
(610) 691–0943

*Sundance Sport
222 East Street
Bloomsburg 17815
(717) 784–0504

Bike Line
26 South Sproul Road
Broomall 19008
(610) 356–3022

Cycles Bikyle
1044 Lancaster Avenue
Bryn Mawr 19010
(215) 525–8442

*Holmes Cycling
2139 Market Street
Camp Hill 17011
(717) 737–3461

*Wildware Outfitters
Camp Hill Mall
Camp Hill 17011
(717) 737–2728

Cole's Bicycles
327 North Hanover Street
Carlisle 17013
(717) 249–3833

Bob's Bicycle
603 Wayne Avenue
Chambersburg 17201
(717) 263–8176

Family Cycling
359 East Washington
Chambersburg 17201
(717) 263–9604

Wheels
2903 Edgemont Avenue
Chester 19015
(610) 876–0971

In Gear Cycling & Fitness
406 East Penn Avenue
Cleona 17042
(717) 273–4477

Suburban Bicycle
2000 Butler Pike
Conshohocken 19428
(610) 828–7557

*Dallas Bike Works
Dallas Shopping Center
Dallas 18612
(717) 675–2616

Cycle Sports, Ltd.
614 Easton Road
Doylestown 18901
(215) 340–2526

Jack's Broken Spoke
110 South Eighteenth Street
Easton 18042
(610) 258–4404

Pocono Gateway Cycle
R.D. 8, Box 8915
East Stroudsburg 18301
(717) 424–1552

Vitulli's Cycle Fit
298 Washington Street
East Stroudsburg 18301
(717) 424–1163

Lancaster Country Cyclery
45 South Market Street
Elizabethtown 17022
(717) 361–8100

*Green Mountain Cyclery
285 South Reading Road
Ephrata 17522
(717) 859–2422

Martin's Bike Shop
1194 Division Highway
Ephrata 17522
(717) 354–9127

*The Crank
512 North Reading Road
Ephrata 17522
(717) 733–8809

Weaver's Bike Shop
240 Sheffers School Road
Ephrata 17522
(717) 656–9385

Bike Line
404 West Lincoln Highway
Exton 19341
(610) 594–9380

Bicycles Unlimited
325 Bustleton Pike
Feasterville 19033
(215) 357–0862

Guy's Bicycles
326 East Street Road
Feasterville 19033
(215) 355–1166

Bike Line
1820 Bethlehem Pike
Flourtown 19031
(215) 233–5499

B&B Bike
112 Shoemaker Street
Forty Fort 18704
(717) 287–3696

*Gettysburg Cycling & Fitness
100 Buford Avenue
Gettysburg 17325
(717) 334–7791

Spokes Bike Shop
R.R. 4
Box 4125
Hamburg 19526
(610) 562–8900

Kessler's Bicycle
129 Baltimore Street
Hanover 17331
(717) 632–9157

Bikesport Bike & Fitness
371 Main Street
Harleysville 19348
(215) 256–6613

Rainbow Cycles
550 North Mountain Road
Harrisburg 17112
(717) 545–0299

The Pedal Pusher
3798 Walnut Street
Harrisburg 17109
(717) 652–7760

Cycles by Ralf
2101 Oakmont Boulevard
Havertown 19083
(610) 449–2730

Pearson Bike Shop
164 South Fifth Street
Hughesville 17737
(717) 584–2365

In Gear Cycling & Fitness
9030 Bridge Road
Hummelstown 17036
(717) 566–0455

Aspen Cycle
2651 Huntingdon Pike
Huntingdon Valley 19006
(215) 938–8481

The Bike House
10 South Pleasant Street
Jacobus 17407
(717) 428–2028

*Blue Mountain Sports
34 Susquehanna Street
Jim Thorpe 18229
(800) 599–4421

*Pocono Whitewater
H.C. 2, Box 2248
Jim Thorpe 18229
(717) 325–3655

*Bikesit
234 East Dekalb Pike
King of Prussia 19406
(610) 265–1225

Main Bike World
414 Market Street
Kingston 18704
(717) 288–8883

Bike Line
117 Rohrerstown Road
Lancaster 17603
(717) 394–8998

Cycle Circle
310 North Queen Street
Lancaster 17603
(717) 295–3193

Lancaster Bicycle Shop
1138 Manheim Pike
Lancaster 17601
(717) 299–9445

*Mt. Gretna Mountain Bikes
1111 Walnut Street
Lebanon 17042
(717) 273–9499

Bushey's Cycling
254 Lowther Street
Lemoyne 17043
(717) 774–7071

The Bicycle Peddler
R.D. 2, Box 125
Lewisburg 17837
(717) 524–4554

*Bicycle World
747 South Broad Street
Lititz 17543
(717) 626–0650

The Bike Gallery
140 East Main Street
Lock Haven 17745
(717) 748–6580

Bike Line
6520 Carlisle Pike
Mechanicsburg 17055
(717) 795–2930

*MLE Cycle Center
Old State/Providence Roads
Media 19063
(610) 565–1771

Ray's Bicycle Center
317 Broad Street
Montoursville 17754
(717) 368–8899

Marty's Bicycle Shop
160 East Water Street
Muncy 17756
(717) 546–3142

Jaikes & Son Bicycle
434 South Market Street
Nanticoke 18634
(717) 735–8000

Mainly Bikes
229 Haverford Avenue
Narberth 19072
(610) 668–2453

Whistle Stop Bike Shop
2 East Franklin Street
New Freedom 17349
(717) 227–0737

Newtown Bicycle Shop
30 North State Street
Newtown 18940
(215) 968–3200

Bikesit
1400 South Trooper Road
Norristown 19403
(610) 539–8393

Bikesit
1987 West Main Street
Norristown 19403
(610) 539–2453

Steve's Bike
140 West Germantown Road
Norristown 19401
(610) 275–4010

Northampton Cyclery
2145 Main Street
Northampton 18067
(610) 261–1234

Performance, Inc.
1776 East Lancaster Avenue
Paoli 19301
(610) 644–8522

*Bike Tech
1234 Locust Street
Philadelphia 19107
(215) 735–1503

*Bustleton Bike
9261 Roosevelt Boulevard
Philadelphia 19114
(215) 671–1910

Bicycle Therapy
2208 South Street
Philadelphia 19145
(215) 735–7849

Bike Addicts
5548 Ridge Avenue
Philadelphia 19128
(215) 487–3006

Bike Line
416 Oaklane Road
Philadelphia 19126
(215) 424–3773

*Erdenheim Bicycle Center
821 Bethlehem Pike
Philadelphia 19118
(215) 233–9545

Philadelphia Bicycles
826 North Broad Street
Philadelphia 19128
(215) 765–9118

*Frankenstein Bike Works
1430 Spruce Street
Philadelphia 19102
(215) 893–0415

Via Bicycle
1134 Pine Street
Philadelphia 19107
(215) 627–3370

*Village Bikes
843 South Second Street
Philadelphia 19147
(215) 336–5911

Wolff Cycle Co.
4311 Lancaster Avenue
Philadelphia 19104
(215) 222–2171

Bike Line
799 State Street
Pottstown 19464
(610) 970–1866

Fronheiser Cycle
23–38 South Eighth Street
Quakertown 18951
(215) 536–3443

Triangle Bicycle
207 Lisa Lane
Reading 19606
(610) 779–9177

Wolverton's Bike Shop
2904 Kutztown Road
Reading 19605
(610) 929–8205

Cycle Sonic
220 Huntingdon Pike
Rockledge 19046
(215) 379–1102

B & H Bikes
44 East King Street
Shippensburg 17257
(717) 532–9624

*Bicycle Center
909 Main Street
South Williamsport 17701
(717) 323–1153

Performance Bike Shop
749 West Sproul Road
Springfield 19064
(610) 690–2971

*Eddie's Bicycles
480 East College Avenue
State College 16801
(814) 234–3111

*New Age Bicycle Sport
229 South Allen Street
State College 16801
(814) 234–2453

The Ski Station
224 East College Avenue
State College 16801
(814) 237–2655

Bike Line
1035 Andrew Drive
West Chester 19380
(610) 692–9589

Bike Line
909 Paoli Pike
West Chester 19380
(610) 436–8984

West Chester Bike Center
1342B West Chester Pike
West Chester 19382
(610) 431–1856

*Full Cycle Bicycle Shop
2510 MacArthur Road
Whitehall 18052
(610) 432–2858

Main Bike World
379 South Main Street
Wilkes-Barre 18703
(717) 824–7433

Stull Brothers
P.O. Box 2487
Wilkes-Barre 18703
(717) 823–9895

Adventure Cycling
4370 West Market Street
York 17404
(717) 792–4400

The Cycle Works
1273 Chimney Rock Road
York 17406
(717) 755–3376

York Cycle Company
337 West Market Street
York 17401
(717) 846–5800

## Bike Clubs and Rail-Trail Organizations

124 West Church Street
Annville 17003
(717)865–3833

Delaware & Lehigh Canal
  National Heritage Corridor
  Commission
10 East Church Street
Bethlehem 18018
(610) 861–9345

Lehigh Wheelmen
P.O. Box 356
Bethlehem 18016
(610) 967–2653

Canton Bike Club
16 East Tioga Street
Canton 17724
(717) 673–5331

Rail-Trail Council/
  Northeast PA
O&W Road Trail
P.O. Box 100
Clifford 18413
(717) 222–3333

Anthracite Bicycle Club
P.O. Box 1218
Conyngham 18219
(717) 788–6963

Wyoming Valley Bike Club
P.O. Box 253
Dallas 18612
(717) 829–7226

Central Bucks Bike Club
5796 Village Lane
Doylestown 18901
(215) 297–5182

Delaware Valley Bicycle Club
P.O. Box 274
Drexel Hill 19026
(610) 259–3327

Pennsylvania Bike Club
P.O. Box 987
Glenside 19038
(215) 885–5128

Hanover Cyclers
129 Baltimore Street
Hanover 17331
(717) 259–7387

Suburban Cyclists Unlimited
P.O. Box 401
Horsham 19044
(215) 675–8167

Lancaster Bicycle Club
P.O. Box 535
Lancaster 17608
(717) 396–9299

White Clay Bicycle Club
321 Indian Town
Landenburg 19350
(610) 255–0799

Williamsport Bicycle Club
1270 East New Road
Linden 17701
(717) 323–2349

Harrisburg Bike Club
1011 Bridge Street
New Cumberland 17070
(717) 561–1647

Bicycle Club of Philadelphia
P.O. Box 30235
Philadelphia 19130
(215) 977–2164

Berks County Bike Club
4624 Pheasant Run
Reading 19606
(610) 582–5705

Brandywine Bicycle Club
P.O. Box 3162
West Chester 19381
(610) 269–6976

Schuylkill River Greenway
  Association (Thun Trail)
970 Old Mill Road
Wyomissing 19610
(610) 372–3916

Schuylkill River Greenway
  Association (Schuylkill River
  Trail)
970 Old Mill Road
Wyomissing 19610
(610) 372–3916

York County Rail–Trail
  Authority (York Heritage
  Trail)
140 East Market Street
York 17403
(717) 848–5500

## Additional Information

For more information on accommodations and additional sightseeing opportunities, obtain a copy of the *Pennsylvania Visitors Guide* by calling (800) VISIT–PA.

For a copy of the *Bicycling Directory of Pennsylvania*, contact Rails to Trails Conservancy, 105 Locust Street, Harrisburg, PA 17101. (717) 238–1717.

Special thanks to
• Pam Haber and Rails to Trails Conservancy
• Charles Rockwell and the Canton Bicycle Club.

# About the Author

Bill Simpson is a writer and an endurance-sport enthusiast. He lives in Lancaster, Pennsylvania, an area that he considers one of the great places in the world for biking. He has ridden tens of thousands of miles on his bike over Lancaster County's farm roads. His biking motto is "Nowhere to go and all day to get there." When he's not biking, he's often running. He has run more than thirty marathons, and his favorite is a Pennsylvania race, God's Country, through the mountains of Potter County. He is the author of *Guide to the Amish Country.*